CONTENDING FOR BREAKTHROUGH
IN THE MIDST OF PAIN AND DISAPPOINTMENT

I0616079

THE PROCESS OF
SUDDENLY

DAVID JOSEPH & MELODY JOSEPH

Published by David and Melody Joseph.

Printed and distributed by Amazon and/or IngramSpark

ISBN: 979-8-218-69001-4 First Edition

Cover design and Interior design by Moonwalker Digital (moonwalkerdigital.com)

DEDICATION

We dedicate this book to the Lord. He has helped us write this book every step of the way. We give God all the glory for the story He is writing.

We also dedicate this book to our children Esther, Nehemiah, Kanaan Asher, Havilah, and future children. Esther, Nehemiah, and Kanaan, you have left a heavenly legacy as you wait to reunite with us. Havilah, it is a joy to raise you and love you. We are forever grateful to be your parents.

Love, Dad & Mom

FOREWORD

Have you ever wondered how certain people can maintain their peace and remain hopeful even though they have been through a great deal of pain and heartache in life? How do some people seem to be able to still smile and look at the "bright side" in their seemingly dismal circumstances? What makes them not crumble and cave to bitterness and depression? You will discover the keys to having this outlook by the authors who penned these pages.

If you have been through the traumatic experiences of a pregnancy loss, infertility, or adoption failure—or possibly all three—you have found a safe and encouraging place to land in the pages of this book. Having personally experienced a stillbirth of my firstborn, Grace, two high-risk (but thankfully successful pregnancies of my healthy girls born prematurely), several adoption failures, and a miscarriage, I can say this book spoke right to my heart. The stories took me on a tender and beautiful journey with Melody and David through the winding road of the physical, emotional, and spiritual battles they faced. They each share from their own perspectives, portions of their story, which will be so helpful for couples who read it together.

The Josephs paint a very realistic picture of what grief and recurring disappointments look like, opening themselves up in a raw account of their story. They wrestle through, never letting go of hope and give insight to how they have conquered fear and the lies the enemy whispered in their ears! They beckon us to fight the good fight and hold on to our faith in Jesus!! They share insights and resources to improve our health and well-being, which is also key to winning battles. There are moments I had goosebumps reading of their incredible breakthrough victories.

Melody and David provide thought-provoking questions to ponder. They also challenge the narratives often spouted in this world and in the church that keep us from entering our "Promised Land" and from discovering our true calling. This is a book where grief meets the gate. You get to choose to stay where you are or bravely take these keys that have been offered and open this gate before you. I, along with the Josephs, invite you to enter the next chapter of your life with a new perspective on your "test"-imony, where the enemy of your soul is no longer a threat. You will have new vision for the future, assured that nothing is impossible with and through Jesus.

Candy McVicar

Co-Author with Dr. Gary Chapman of *Holding on to Love After You've Lost a Baby: The 5 Love Languages® for Grieving Parents*

Co-Founder and Executive Director of The Missing GRAC Foundation

INTRODUCTION

Throughout history and our lives, there are moments when everything changes. We've experienced it, watched it, heard about it, and read about it in the history books, especially in the Bible. When Abraham and Sarah had Isaac, everything changed at that moment—for them and the rest of human history! When the dove brought Noah back an olive leaf, everything changed instantly. When David slain Goliath, his story (and Israel's story) changed forever.

Most importantly, when our Lord and Savior, Jesus Christ, took on flesh and was born into this world through a virgin, everything was altered! The world was never the same again. And when He died, was resurrected, ascended into Heaven, and gave us a better helper (the Holy Spirit), things were forever different! Our prayer is that you will encounter God through this book and experience healing—and that you will never be the same again.

These are powerful *kairos* moments when lives, families, communities, churches, cities, nations, and the world change instantly! (Kairos is the Greek word meaning "the right or critical moment.")[1] One word. One breath. One prayer. One breakthrough. At just the right time.

One of the many names for our God is Jehovah Perazim. It means "Lord of the breakthroughs."[2] Our God is a God of the suddenly. In one moment, He wants to, can, and does change things for you and me. The Lord wants to step in with signs, wonders, and miracles that glorify His name. If we let Him into our story, our mess, our pain, our dreams, our promises—all of it—He will come through. I can't promise you what that

[1]Introduction

"Kairos," Wikipedia, accessed February 11, 2025, https://en.wikipedia.org/wiki/Kairos.
[2]"2 Samuel 5:20 - Two Victories Over the Philistines," Bible Hub, accessed March 24, 2025, https://biblehub.com/2_samuel/5-20.htm.

will look like. I refuse to put God in a box.

I wish I could tell you when it will happen, but if I've learned anything through it all, being convinced that it will happen is more important than knowing when! If we can be absolutely convinced it will happen, the "when" becomes much less critical. It's surrender, and it is trust. However, it's that time between being convinced that a breakthrough is coming and seeing it through where most of us live our days. It's the tension of contending for something already won without seeing the W in the win column. I believe this is where God does some of His best work. He works in us and on us until we have the capacity to possess and steward the promise! This is the process of the suddenly! What are you contending for?

Chapter 1
SEARING PAIN

Hope deferred makes the heart sick, but a dream fulfilled is a tree of life.

—Proverbs 13:12 NLT

Pain has a funny way of searing memories into our minds, hearts, and souls. The old saying, don't touch the oven when it's hot, is fundamental in our emotional, spiritual, and relational lives too. Once you encounter deep pain, trauma even, it gets seared into the fiber of who you are like you just touched the hot stove. You never want to do it again. This is a helpful kind of pain. It is a pain that teaches you not to do something dangerous. It's your choice not to encounter that pain again. Then there is pain that seems to find you because we live in a fallen world. Sometimes, it has nothing to do with your choices; it just comes out of nowhere and leaves you reeling. It leaves you feeling stuck, not knowing what to do with it.

We walked through a season like that. Some things are hard to revisit even as we put these words to paper, but we know God works everything out for our good (Rom. 8:28). He does not cause hurt and harm to happen to us. That is always us or the adversary. However, no matter what, God always has the last word! God uses anything and everything to make us like Him and to glorify Him! For us, we have a choice. We can allow real emotions to make us bitter, envious, hostile, defeated, or whatever negative emotion you want to insert there. Or we can look at pain as an invitation.

We realized later in our journey that this intense pain was and is an invitation. It's an invitation to climb into our heavenly Father's lap and give it all to Him. He made a beautiful exchange for us at Calvary. He took our pain on Himself! He took it in His body, mind, emotions, and Spirit. We undermine Christ's sacrifice when we hold on to our painful situations. Pain comes in waves, but Jesus already took it all for us! Give it to Him now. Please don't waste another second holding on to it. He already took the punishment and the questions. The answers aren't in the world; they are in Jesus! Pain is an invitation to share in the sufferings of Christ so that we might become more intimate with Him. He makes beauty from ashes. He brings hope into the darkest of situations. He supernaturally empowers us to love and forgive others in the middle of our pain, like He did for us. Invite Him in. Pain is an invitation.

Loss (David) ✳

I had experienced pain before. I had lost wrestling matches, baseball games, pets, and even great friends. Nothing compares to the pain of losing a child. It goes against the natural order of things. Losing grandparents and parents is hard; I would never try to diminish that. As hard as it is to admit, those are natural occurrences. In a sense, it is supposed to happen that way. Losing a child is losing a part of who you are. It's losing legacy, dreams, and a future that I felt God had ordained. I couldn't imagine willingly watching a child die like our Father God did. It feels like your world stops, your hope stops, and your future is gone—or at least you are missing a massive part of it! The sear of pain, if you will, started for us on October 1, 2017. I remember the moments, the sights, the sounds, the feelings, the details, all of it.

I love the Minnesota Vikings. I was born and raised in a small town in central Minnesota. Some of my best early memories are watching the 1998 Vikings go 15-1 while Randy Moss came on the scene and changed the

2

game of football forever. It was a constant in my life. Faith (go to church), family (I shared this with my dad and other family and friends), and football (every Sunday)! We usually got Chinese food and watched the games in our basement. If you know anything about the Vikings, you know I've also endured plenty of heartbreak with that passion! Call me crazy, but God speaks to me through my passions. He often uses the Vikings, among other things like hunting, the outdoors, wrestling, work, and family. He meets me in my passions and cares about what I care about. I digress.

October 1, 2017, was a Sunday. The Vikings were playing the Lions at US Bank Stadium. My dad and I had tickets on the turf through a work colleague! As you can imagine, I was beyond excited. I also had another exciting thing happening. My wife, Melody, was pregnant with our first daughter. It was our first child, who we later named Esther, and we were naive about the fragility of pregnancy in its early stages. Melody started having symptoms of miscarriage, and I took her to the hospital instead of going to the game.

I remember feeling helpless as we prayed and contended for a breakthrough. I watched the game from a hospital room with Melody in lots of emotional and physical pain. The doctor walked in during a critical game drive. At a moment that already felt like the greatest torment I could experience, he delivered the news in a cold, matter-of-fact manner: "I'm sorry, but there is no heartbeat." At that exact moment, Dalvin Cook suffered a season-ending ACL injury, fumbled the ball, and the Vikings lost. It was a day of tremendous loss. Our dreams and future were altered in a moment of darkness and pain. We cried in each other's arms, and now we had to break the news to friends and family. We had love and support from many, but similar to a football season, for most, it was on to the next week, so to speak. Our world stopped. The rest of the world kept going.

The pain was like nothing I had ever experienced. Watching my young wife go through the physical part was heartbreaking. But the physical pain doesn't compare to the nothingness—the emptiness you feel. I found myself longing for eternity. I know my daughter is with Jesus in Heaven. I rejoice over that fact, but I've struggled with the why. Why can't I experience the joy of fathering her here on earth? I remember feeling purposeless. I knew my purpose was to be a father! What was the point of all this if I couldn't be that? It was a dark place. We clung to the hope we have in Jesus and the fact that miscarriages are common. Doctors advised us to try again, and we didn't know any better! We've since learned much more that we will share, but at the time, like the Vikings, we recovered from the loss and looked to the next game (if you will).

I've always been passionate about health, wellness, and performance. I grew up competing in athletics in high school and college. I loved it. I loved it because it was tough for me, and it stretched me. I wasn't the most gifted athlete. I grew up having to overcome a lot of challenges, including premature birth, asthma, allergies, and just a general lack of balance and coordination. Because of that, I developed a passion for strength training, fitness, wellness, nutrition, recovery, and biohacking. I dove in to get every edge I could and saw some miraculous breakthroughs that came through supernatural and natural means. It just became a part of me and extended to Melody as we grew in love and marriage.

Early in our marriage, we felt we had good guidance and plans regarding fertility. We will get into more specifics later, but for the story's sake, know that we left no stone unturned in our quest for health, wellness, and fertility. We went both medical and natural routes. We did all the testing and then some. We received treatment all over the country. We built a new home due to mold exposure. We did anything and everything that could optimize our health and family!

In July of 2018, we lost our first son to another early miscarriage. We later named him Nehemiah. The loss of Esther seared into my brain. As I've shared, I remember every detail. The loss of Nehemiah was numbing. My brain blacked it out. I do not remember much of it. I couldn't even imagine that this would happen to us again! All the same feelings came flooding back. The pain that we experienced emotionally, spiritually, and physically was palpable. The most painful part was the sobering reality that this had happened twice in a row. Naturally, there were questions a young couple in their twenties never want to ask: Will parenthood ever happen for us? Are we broken? Are there significant issues with us? Does God care? Does He see us? I thought that babies were God's idea. We lived in purity and health, and I can't do justice to the pain and questions we had at that moment. I was numb. A part of me died that day again.

At that point, we felt we were not getting the answers we needed from doctors. We got little more than the standard, "Just try again; miscarriages are common." In our spirits, we knew there was more and that this stuff wasn't supposed to happen in God's perfect design. We believe it shouldn't exist here if it doesn't exist in Heaven. We knew deep down that our experience should and would match God's words over our lives, but we weren't seeing it yet.

What's Wrong? (Melody)

As we neared two and a half years into our marriage, we decided to start a family. We felt we had taken the first couple of years of our marriage to establish our relationship with each other, and we were ready to add to our family. In August 2017, we got pregnant with our first child. We later named her Esther. I carried her for eight weeks and then had a miscarriage.

We were devastated. Our innocence of not knowing what can go wrong in pregnancy was gone. We never thought it would happen to us, but here we were. We took a break to let my body heal. We made some adjustments and got pregnant seven months later because we really wanted a baby. Devastatingly again, we miscarried. Our son Nehemiah was also only with us for eight short weeks. I remember, through tears, having David read Scripture to help me focus on something other than the all-encompassing pain that was happening. It was the only thing that helped me through it.

Again, loss and grief set in for us. It was a confusing journey as to why I couldn't carry a baby to term. Why couldn't we start a family? Isn't it a desire God wants to bring to pass? So many questions ran through our minds. It was time to take a step back and process.

When you lose someone, it echoes in every area of your life. The physical, mental, emotional, and spiritual parts of you are all affected. It was hard for us to start a family, and it was not going as we had hoped. We learned that one in four pregnancies can end in loss. I asked the question, "Why me?" Why us? It hurt so much because we had loved so deeply. Why wasn't it happening if our bodies were designed to create life? We went on a long journey with the Lord as we asked these questions.

The desire for children was a driving force in our lives during that season. Because of that, we decided to investigate the root causes of what my body was going through.

An Obedient Word (David) ✶ ──────────────────

We sought the Lord, and we felt peace trying a more natural and holistic approach to healing and growing our family. We have nothing against the medical field, and there are certainly times when our Western medical model can save lives. They absolutely help people with advanced technologies, drugs, and techniques. However, we ended up getting frustrated with medical fertility specialists because their only answers were, "Try again," and drugs or medication.

We connected with some wonderful people and approaches to health throughout our journey. Still, we ended up finding a myriad of things that could have been contributing to infertility and loss, and we attacked them with every ounce of energy, prayer, finances, and hope that we had. I hope this doesn't sound discouraging, but it took us a couple of years to naturally detox, heal, change our diet, and finally get the lab testing numbers to an appropriate level for a healthy pregnancy. We will describe this in more detail later in this book, but for the sake of the big picture story, know if there was anything out there that could help, we tried it!

We had, and still have, a solid support system. Our families live in the same state, and we can reach out whenever we need help. Our church family and community are tried and true; they've been with us through thick and thin. We are always encouraged by prayer, intercession, and even people just reaching out quickly, asking us how we are doing and how they can support us. We and others going through things like this often don't need anything tangible. We need to feel cared for and seen. We need to know that people also remember and acknowledge our sons and daughters. Many times, that's all it takes.

It's a matter of perspective. Every pregnancy announcement was a bittersweet moment, but a handful of people still saw us and reached out. It kept us going. Do not underestimate the power of a quick text message. For us, just knowing we crossed someone's mind and heart in prayer encouraged us that we would make it through. There was one message in particular that marked us forever. In the fall of 2020, our dear friend and mentor received a vision from the Lord for us and encouraged us with it. We received a prophetic promise from God about having babies.

I love God's voice. Matthew 4:4 (TPT) says, "Bread alone will not satisfy, but true life is found in every word that constantly goes forth from God's mouth." I love it when God speaks through His Scripture. When I talk about the prophetic, it's important to say up front that it in NO way devalues or dishonors Scripture. The Bible is the foundation. God's Word is alive, and He speaks through it, AND (I won't say but) His Holy Spirit is in us, and He speaks to us through impressions, whispers, pictures, dreams, visions, prophets, prophetic people, situations, nature, music, and a myriad of ways.

We are passionate about His voice because it has kept us hanging on and moving forward in some of life's most confusing and dark times. He's encouraged, directed, provided, and corrected us in the most loving ways possible.

On that particular fall day in 2020, our friend was obedient in sharing what God was saying about our family. Receiving that word nourished our spirits, minds, hearts, bodies, and will! We knew in that moment that God saw us, loved us, and, most importantly, would get the last word in our story.

Reflection:

What is one painful experience you have gone through that has shaped you for better or worse?

Prayer:

Lord, I ask You to draw near to me right now. I am going through something painful, and I want to see who You are amid my circumstances. Comfort me as You reveal Yourself. In Jesus's name, I pray. Amen.

Chapter 2
OUR PROMISED LAND

Now the Lord said to Abram,

"Go from your country,

And from your relatives

And from your father's house,

To the land which I will show you;

And I will make you into a great nation,

And I will bless you,

And make your name great;

And you shall be a blessing;

And I will bless those who bless you,

And the one who curses you I will curse.

And in you all the families of the earth will
be blessed."

—Genesis 12:1–3 NASB

The prophetic word from our friend was more than an encouragement. It was a turning point. It was the dawning of a new season. Much like Abram and Sarai, it was a calling for us to leave some things behind and, with faith, to GO. Go where? We didn't know yet. What would the journey look like? We didn't have those answers.

Our Promised Land (David) ✳━━━━━━━━━━━━━━━━

In Genesis 12:1, God asks Abram to leave it all behind. He instructs him to leave all that is familiar. God asks him to leave his hometown and his way of life. The original Hebrew used here is *lech-lecha*, which is literally translated as "go to yourself,"[3] but the implication of the phrase is something like "go find yourself." I'm taking some liberties, but it seems God is challenging Abram at this moment. If Abram is willing to obey and leave the familiar behind, God planned to bless him with more than he could imagine. It's similar to the New Testament call in Matthew 16:25, where Jesus explains to believers that we inherit more of the kingdom life when we give up our comforts and way of life to follow Him!

I believe that our God is so kind. He knew what was best for Abram, and He knows what is best for you and me. Yet, in the mystery of it all, He still asks for our involvement. Our response to God's promises must be yes and amen! The first step in them coming to pass is for us to come into alignment and believe in the promise and the promise giver. In Genesis 12, God gives Abram and Sarai just enough encouragement to take one step. He provides them with nourishment for the season they are in and asks for their trust. They didn't know what was coming next, but they ultimately knew that all nations would be blessed through them (Gen. 12:3)!

3

Chapter Two

Michael M. Cohen, "What does the 'lech lecha' phrase mean?" The Jerusalem Post, published Dec 2020, https://www.jpost.com/judaism/torah-portion/lecha-lecha-and-prayer-647471.

We don't need to understand what's next when we know how the story ends. I liken this idea to football because it's how my simple brain works. I've already said that I love cheering on the Minnesota Vikings. It's been a tradition in our family for as long as I can remember. As a fan, I want them to win the game. I don't care how it happens as long as it happens. I often think to myself: If I knew the outcome of the game was a win, I wouldn't get so worked up and emotional during the roller coaster of the game. If they were down by four scores, I'd sit back on the couch and embrace the comeback that was on its way!

In much more consequential matters, God was kind to Abram in this way. He was this kind to Melody and me. The prophetic promise that we referenced at the end of chapter 1 was our Genesis 12 moment. We knew God's heart, we knew the promise, and we knew the outcome; we just had NO idea what was coming next. Sometimes, God gives us prophetic words because He knows we are going to need something to hold on to. He doesn't always stop bad things from happening to good people, but He always provides enough nourishment for the day and the season. He is faithful in giving us daily bread and walking through life with us in a manner that is for our good and His glory!

Like Abram and Sarai, Melody and I just took the next step. I've noticed that many times in my walk with God, He gives me just enough to take one step. He doesn't always reveal the entire parade—He wants us to have enough faith to co-labor with Him and take the next step together.

After a while, we decided to discontinue some of the detoxing and healing modalities that wouldn't be a good idea for conception and pregnancy, and just a few months after we got that sweet encouragement from the Lord, we found out we were pregnant! We were delighted and just amazed. Of course, some natural fears and anxieties accompanied us from past losses, but the Holy Spirit kept reminding us of His word and faithfulness. We made it to eight weeks, and that was a breakthrough in and of itself. Our joy and confidence in the Lord were uncontainable! We made it to twelve weeks. We found out our baby was a boy! We did a gender reveal with our families, which was the first time we got to do that. We named him Kanaan as a reference to the biblical promised land. He was our promised land, and we were growing so excited for his arrival.

Then, we made it to twenty weeks! It was indeed a supernatural pregnancy. Melody was feeling great and doing such a good job. Her hormone levels were good, and we began to feel his kicks and wiggles. I remember some of the sweetest moments we spent together before bed praying and worshiping, just the three of us, as Kanaan would join with outbursts of praise and worship from his cozy hiding place. He got to experience some amazing things with us. Kanaan was there as his daddy coached the local high school wrestling team to its first and only state championship! He was a junior groomsman at his auntie and uncle's wedding, and Daddy got to officiate it. He went on vacation with us to beautiful Door County. Melody and I got the nursery ready, went shopping for clothes, and had a wonderful baby shower. The big day was fast approaching as we neared the thirty-five-week mark of a pregnancy that seemed perfect and healthy to our knowledge.

Living a Nightmare (David) ✳ ━━━━━━━━━━━━━━━━━━

Another one of my passions is archery hunting. We like hunting deer and turkey here in Minnesota, but one of the most incredible experiences of my entire life is archery hunting elk in Colorado! It was early September, and I had an elk hunt planned with some family and friends. I went to a routine midwife appointment with Melody just before we left to ensure everything would be good for a week or so and that there'd be no surprises. It was a joyous and happy occasion. The three of us in the room were lighthearted, going through routine things and discussing the delivery plan. Melody jumped up on the table for some measurements, and suddenly, our whole life changed.

Our midwife was trying so hard to stay positive and not scare us, but the panic in her eyes gave it away. Kanaan was measuring very small, and she was concerned that he hadn't grown much. We knew he was alive and well because we could feel him moving and enjoying his day. We felt anything but joy. We felt terrified. However, we stayed positive, praying and declaring God's word over Kanaan's life.

We then had to go in for a series of tests and ultrasounds. I remember the first one. The tech was pleasant, but she didn't say much. We got a picture of Kanaan giving us a "thumbs up" that we still cherish today. That gave us a reason to muster a smile in the middle of the tears. The tech sent everything to the doctor, and we went on our way. We were grabbing lunch before another appointment, and our midwife called. I answered, and immediately, Melody's face was white, peeked, and blotchy. She heard our midwife's voice. Tears rolled down her face as I silently handed the phone to her. I don't remember much of the rest of that day. The numbness returned. It was like we were living in a nightmare. I looked at Melody, and we threw our food away. We got up to walk to the car, and I heard the most unthinkable words you could imagine: "The doctor believes your son has a rare condition called Trisomy 13. It's incompatible with life."

Crushing News (Melody) ✳━━━━━━━━━━━━━━━━━━

After the loss of our first two babies, we leaned into the Lord in the following months and let His peace cover us. We discovered some things about our health, and over the next couple of years, we worked on many areas, including our hormones, gut, toxins, diet, etc. In short, we found we had massive mold exposure that affected our bodies, specifically our immune response. It could have even influenced our previous losses, but we will never know for sure.

As our health improved, I got pregnant in January 2021. It was such an exciting time for us, but it was also nerve-wracking. As weeks passed, and we surpassed the eight-week mark, we decided to wait until week twelve to tell our families. Because of the prior losses, I had to test my hormones weekly to make sure things were where they should be. I had no doubt in my mind that this child was a miracle, and we could not wait to meet him. We had waited so long, and finally, it was happening. Being pregnant and experiencing kicks and movement was such a joy. Every night, David got to feel him kick. It was miraculous.

At my thirty-four-week appointment, our midwife noticed I had not gotten bigger. When she measured me, she immediately looked concerned. She mentioned I was measuring small and that I needed to have an ultrasound. As a background, we had decided not to do any prior genetic testing or ultrasounds because we were going to love this baby no matter what. In our minds, there was no way that there was anything wrong, but her concerns were viable.

The next day, we went in for a regular ultrasound. As the tech checked things, she was quiet. I asked, but she was not allowed to tell me any details. She only said that the baby was small for my gestation but that he might be a small baby. We left that ultrasound not resolved, but we had hope that nothing major was wrong.

The next day, we got a call that we needed to do a more in-depth ultrasound because they were seeing things that were concerning. Again, we went in; this time, we did not have the best tech. She had no friendly bedside manner at all. As she checked our son, she rattled off multiple things that were wrong:

Six fingers.

Six toes.

Small eyes.

One kidney.

Hole in heart.

Brain not developed (The halves were there, but there was nothing in the middle).

Double Cleft lip and palate.

Small head and more.

My head was spinning. I was utterly silent, with tears pouring down my face. It was a complete shock, and I was not prepared to hear those descriptions. Finally, the lady looked over and said, "Oh, do you want me to stop?" She was very insensitive.

That crushing news began a deep heartache and a struggle to hold onto hope. We left that appointment completely helpless. We were worried, fearful, sad, shocked, and in denial. We were in such a state of shock that what we were just told didn't seem true. We really did not know what would happen next.

As we left that appointment, I was supposed to go to the dentist that day, so we headed in that direction. We stopped for lunch, placed our order, and sat down. My cell phone was in my purse, and I noticed I had a missed call from our midwife. David's phone rang. I was in the middle of eating as he picked it up. His face changed immediately as our midwife began to explain what they were seeing from the ultrasounds. I immediately lost my appetite. I already knew it wasn't good. David handed me the phone. She began to explain a condition that they believed our son had: Trisomy 13. I was still shocked. She described the defects and how they would not change because they happen at conception. She felt terrible but let us know it wasn't our fault. She said they wanted me to go back the next day to discuss a plan of action and let her know the next steps. She would be there for us no matter our decision regarding how we would give birth to our son.

We left the restaurant and drove home. That drive was an emotionally confusing one. We didn't know what to do. We had to tell our families, but how?

We got home, and all I wanted to do was lie down and cry. Our dogs tried to console us as we sobbed and prayed for a miracle. I was so distraught I decided to reach out to some friends in my community who prayed with me. Someone messaged me and sent me the testimony of her child, who had many issues while in the womb that would not let the child survive. But her little girl was now nine years old, thriving and doing better than the doctors would have guessed. I held onto that testimony. It gave me hope from God that He still wanted to heal our son and certainly could do it. It would take a miracle. We prayed over him as if he was already healed. It was the only thing that kept us from constantly going into a bottomless pit of despair.

A Change of Plans (Melody) ✳━━━━━━━━━━━━━━━

The next day, we went to the hospital. A doctor, a geneticist, and a palliative care counselor met us at different times in a cold, stale room. It was hard for me to believe that this was our reality. Our son, still kicking and moving around inside at that moment, made me feel like I was protecting him, and maybe he could have more time to grow so defects could be healed and go away. But that was an impossible dream.

The doctor first sat down with us and went over what they believed our son had: Trisomy 13. To confirm this and discuss how and when delivery would happen, we had to know what we were dealing with. He said I needed to do an amniocentesis. I paused. I remembered looking that up at the beginning of pregnancy and decided I would never do that procedure because of the high risk of miscarriage. Unfortunately, this was the only way they could confirm his condition. I was given no other options. The next day, it would have to be done. I was so scared I would lose our son. The doctor continued saying this condition was "incompatible with life" and that we had the option to let him die now if we wanted. I was shocked and taken back in my seat. I could never imagine doing that to our son. It was against what I believed. I would let him be born when he and my body were ready and hopefully get to see him alive before he passed.

The other two specialists came inside the cold white room. The geneticist was not cordial or sensitive. She said things as a matter of fact, and that rubbed me raw. She said our son's condition was the rarest of Trisomy 13, which meant there was no chance of survival. She recommended we look at the palliative care folder she gave us. Palliative care meant keeping him comfortable after birth until he passed away. I could not even look at or open the folder. The counselor took time to talk with us and validate how we were feeling. However, she couldn't change our situation.

We went home knowing we had to tell our families what was happening. My family was in different areas, so we needed to make phone calls and let them know. David's family lived close, so they came over to our house. I remember it being one of the worst feelings. Everyone was in shock, perplexed, and sad for us. Amidst all this, David was supposed to leave for his elk hunt in a couple of days, but those plans now changed.

The next day, we went in for the amniocentesis. I remember feeling I needed to be brave. I was so scared, but I knew I had to be brave for my son. Our situation had taken a turn for the worse, and there was nothing else we could do. God would have to do a miracle. It didn't matter what I had done during my pregnancy or now tried to do because Trisomy 13 happens at conception.

I remember being so afraid, but David and I prayed for peace to be with us during the procedure. As the doctor described what he was doing, I asked some questions. Kanaan moved around so much that the doctor had to be extremely careful when taking the amniotic fluid sample. When he took the sample, I asked how that would affect Kanaan. The doctor wasn't too worried, thought he would be fine, and said my body should produce more amniotic fluid.

It was Labor Day weekend, so we had a couple of days before we would get results back. It was tough to be around family and friends. Everyone else was enjoying themselves and each other's company. Knowing what was going on with our son hurt so much that I couldn't focus on anything else.

As the weekend passed, we prayed and prayed and declared until we couldn't anymore. We were desperate for a miracle—a solution, a healing. We still believed that God could heal Kanaan and bring a miracle. We decided to play mini golf on Labor Day and get outside in the fresh air. It was enjoyable, but as we drove home, I realized I was having a lot of back pain. I didn't think much of it until it continued through the night. My body had already started having contractions. Since I have a relatively high pain tolerance, I tried to ignore the pain through the night. The next day, I realized I had not felt our son kick the day before, which was not normal for him. This alarmed me, so I called my midwife. The amnio results were not in, but I feared something was wrong.

We hurried in to meet her at the birth center, and she checked for his heartbeat. Silence filled the room. There was no heartbeat. Tears flowed as she left and gave us space to cry. We held each other as our reality set in. After some time, she came in, and my body was already starting to prepare for labor. We had to discuss our plan for birth and care after we had Kanaan. After talking with our midwife, I felt peace about delivering at the birth center. It was more intimate and comfortable than the stale hospital. I was confident God would help me birth Kanaan without all the interventions.

As we left, we said we would contact her if things started to change or progress. Kanaan had most likely passed away the day before (a couple of days after the amniocentesis). We grabbed lunch on our way home and updated our parents. I got my birthing bag packed and ready to go. After a short while, my body started going into labor at home, and I worked through the contractions. We had dinner with some family early in the evening. My contractions started to get closer together, so we headed to the birth center and called our midwife. I remember the night like it was yesterday. It was dark outside and lightning. The lightning lit up the sky as we drove. I was surprised I could handle the contractions so well on the ride.

I had called one of my sisters that day and asked if she could be my doula and be there with me. She said yes, of course she would. She met us at the birth center.

We arrived and set up in a dimly lit room with a warm bathtub. I labored as David played worship music and prayed. As things intensified quickly, I got scared. Fear filled my mind. "What will our son look like? Will

I be afraid to see him? Can I actually do this?" It was all happening so fast. I cried out to God and asked Him to give me peace and a pain-free delivery. He gave me a vision at that moment, right before I birthed Kanaan. In the vision, Kanaan told me he was okay and was already with Jesus. I started to cry.

Our midwife prayed, and with a few pushes, I delivered our son. The midwife took our son to examine him and wrap him up before we saw him. A wave of shock and sadness suddenly overtook me. There were no cries and no happy tears—just emptiness. Yes, God had given me peace through it, but it was so unbelievably hard. This picture was not what I had imagined when I first found out I was pregnant, but Kanaan Asher Joseph came into the world weighing three pounds at 11:27 p.m. on September 7, 2021. Our lives forever changed.

When the midwife brought Kanaan in, it was so quiet. She wrapped him in a towel, and I remember David and I unwrapping him very slowly. I was nervous to see his appearance as the hospital had scared me with their descriptions. There he was, imperfect in the world's eyes but perfect to me. He was a precious gift I had gotten to carry into my third trimester. It was a shock holding him, seeing him, and realizing this was our reality. I felt weak, hurt, sad, and shocked. It didn't feel real. We were stuck in a living nightmare.

The time with him was too short. It went too fast, and it was hard to absorb everything happening. The moment we had to leave him and head to the hospital was the hardest. I regretted not having enough pictures and keepsakes and not having my parents there. Everything happened so fast that I didn't know how to handle it. We knew we had a long journey ahead as we got home late the next morning, exhausted. The days, months, and years after changed who we have become, and we value each moment God gives us in this life. More than ever, we realized we needed guidance in healing, processing, grieving, and leaning into God.

Questions (David) ✳

We were crushed, devastated, and confused after losing Kanaan. It was unthinkable pain. The why questions filled my mind and lips. How could this happen now after all we've done and been through? Does God really speak? Did God say what we thought He said? Can we trust God? Is God good? If He is, why this, why us, and why now?

We knew God's will in this area of our lives, but the current reality felt like the polar opposite of where we thought we'd be. Instead of taking care of my son, changing his diapers, and having nights up with a crying baby, I was taking care of my son's gravesite, changing the flowers by his headstone, and Melody and I were crying ourselves to sleep. I'm yearning for the restoration of all things and the return of Jesus. I can't wait to meet our children, who are waiting for us. And I'm excited to talk to Abram and Sarai. We'll continue their story throughout the book. I believe they felt the same way we did. They received a promise of future children, but their lives looked like the opposite. Even though they were imperfect (like us), God kept encouraging them with a fresh word to nudge them to take one more step.

Our journey of grief was much like that. Although it was far from a linear progression, and you never really get over or move on from losing a child, we had to cling to the Holy Spirit, climb in the Father's lap, and let our frustration invite us into a deeper union and understanding of Him and His ways.

Reflection:

~   In your pain or grief, did you have moments when you
    asked God why?

~   Are there specific times you felt hopeless?

Prayer:

Lord, help me be a supportive friend, relative, coworker,
or neighbor to the person I know who is going through pain
right now. Show me ways I can support them and love them. Be
with them as they go through this hard time. Bring healing in
every way. In Jesus's name, I pray. Amen.

Chapter 3
GRIEVING WITH HOPE

But we do not want you to be uninformed,
brothers and sisters, about those who are
asleep, so that you will not grieve as indeed
the rest of mankind do, who have no hope.

—1 Thessalonians 4:13 NASB

Grief is an unwelcome intruder in our lives. It comes when you least expect it, takes everything you thought you knew about life, and shatters it. It's like walking around with a weighted vest on in your everyday life. It is the most profound ache you could imagine. Grief is so isolating because our culture doesn't do an excellent job of acknowledging it after the funeral. We are expected to move on and avoid uncomfortable topics. To be honest, we were more like that before we went through the horrific and shocking losses of our children. After that, we couldn't just move on. Our whole world stopped, and the rest of the world kept spinning. Parts of us had died. We were different, but the people around us expected us to be the same as before the tragedy. We weren't sure if we'd ever be the same again.

Jesus Changes Everything (David)

It was hard to enjoy anything without considering that our children weren't here to experience that part of life with us. Our hope and future seemed to have been taken, destroyed, and altered. It's hard to describe how dark, desperate, and lonely that grief is. Friends and family are needed support systems. I would never try to diminish that or appear like I didn't appreciate the visits, texts, calls, gifts, meals, etc. Melody and I appreciated them so much, and they kept us going. Even so, if you've been in that pit of grief, you know even that best friend goes back to his or her life. Even the most well-intended and loving relative had other things to focus on and other babies to love.

We didn't. Although we had support and love, humans have limited capacity. Eventually, we were left to cry alone when everyone else seemingly returned to their routines, children, jobs, churches, communities, or what have you. Grief struck others, but it stuck to us like an infected tick. We couldn't get out of it, and the side effects were hopelessness, depression, bitterness, envy, and striving. Grief leaves you feeling helpless. I would have given everything I had to change the circumstances, but I couldn't. There was simply nothing I could do, and as a type A, results-oriented person, that was nauseating to live with!

As I sit here and write this, I don't feel like words can bring the deep despairs of grief any justice. If you've been in that pit, you know. Maybe memories are flooding back to you as you read this. I wish I could say that there is a magic bullet to get through the sting of grief. If there is, I haven't found it. *I believe there are simply no shortcuts to any place worth going.* All I can offer you is this: I don't know how anyone gets through these seasons without Jesus. The Bible says, "But we do not want you to be uninformed, brothers, about those who are asleep, that you may not grieve as others do who have no hope" (1 Thess. 4:13 ESV).

Jesus changes everything. With the hope that Jesus offers, we can do life differently. We can grieve differently, and we can be eternally different! Losing a child, or any loved one for that matter, can make you long for Heaven. I found glimmers of hope when I'd dream about seeing my children again without pain or disease. God has repeatedly reassured us that our babies are healthy, whole, and thriving more than they ever could have here. Still, it seems unfair. If God is eternal, why didn't He let us enjoy the kids for a while on earth? Even in the reprieve, there were and are questions.

All Things New (David) ✸ ————————————————

I still remember a moment when I was sitting in a church office receiving counseling, and I was talking, crying, and dreaming about this very thing—our children who are in God's presence but not ours. God has been so merciful and kind in my most tender moments. In my darkest grief, He painted a vision before me as I closed my eyes. It was like He took me to Heaven; although I wasn't physically there, it felt like a virtual reality dream. I saw the vibrant colors, the streets of gold, and the heroes we dream about meeting.

Most importantly, though, He took me to a place that looked like a national park in high definition! There were rugged mountains, streams of living water, rainbows, exotic and heavenly creatures, and a quiet, clear mountain lake. I saw three beautiful children in their completely restored bodies. They were laughing, running, swimming, and fishing. Jesus Himself was there teaching them and giving them His undivided attention. It hit me: It was Kanaan, Esther, and Nehemiah that He was showing me. I lost it in emotion! I didn't want to leave, yet there was a tangible peace as palpable as I've ever felt that they were thriving and serving in their unique assignments. That encounter changed me, marked me, and set my grief journey on a trajectory that could end in restoration and joy. It didn't happen instantly, but that vision made the process possible. God made joy and peace accessible in that moment when they weren't accessible previously!

I can't talk about grief without discussing Heaven and God's plan to restore everything to His original design. If we're being honest, I think we all ache for that day. That encounter set Melody and me on a journey to learn more about Heaven and God's ultimate plan because I realized

I had some views from my childhood that weren't rooted in hope! Steve Backlund of Igniting Hope Ministries wisely states, "Every area of your life that doesn't glisten with hope means you are believing a lie."[4] I was believing a lie or at least a partial truth about Heaven. I was raised in the nineties, and we had the Left Behind series and lots of teaching about the rapture and the tribulation. There was so much focus on the fear of going to Hell that it essentially just made me afraid of the future events I read about throughout Scripture. I'm not trying to say that those teachings are entirely untrue; I'm simply saying the emphasis didn't help shape hope in my life. It shaped an anemic, "Just don't be bad" approach to my relationship with Jesus and eternity.

To make matters worse for my psyche, I was also taught that Heaven was just an eternal worship service and that we wouldn't care about anything we care about here anymore. Again, while there may be elements of truth in these statements, it left me reeling and depressed in my grieving state. I had no hope for the future because I thought everything would burn, and I wouldn't recognize people and places in Heaven anyway. It took the tragic passing of my kids to spur me deeper into the studies of Scripture on the topic of eternity, Heaven, and the ultimate plan of our Savior to restore all things and make all things new! Matthew 19:28–29 says:

✱ Jesus said to them, "Truly I tell you, at the renewal of all things, when the Son of Man sits on his glorious throne, you who have followed me will also sit on twelve thrones, judging the twelve tribes of Israel. And everyone who has left houses or brothers or sisters or father or mother or wife or children or fields for my sake will

4

Chapter Three

Igniting Hope Ministries, "Glistening Hope Part 1," December 7, 2015, https://www.youtube.com/watch?v=ILDH8119H-U.

receive a hundred times as much and will inherit eternal life.

The original word (palingenesia) translated renewal means a new birth or recreation.[5] It carries the idea of something being restored to its original state. Jesus is saying here that God will restore Eden at the renewal of all things. All of His creation is going to be restored to the original intent, which God said is good! Also in Scripture, we see "He who was seated on the throne said, 'Behold, I am making all things new'" (Rev. 21:5 ESV).

I love John Eldredge's book All Things New. His work was instrumental in encouraging Melody and me to these truths. Eldredge highlights that God is not necessarily making new things. He's making all things new![6] That means that when Jesus comes back, and we go home, we will recognize people, places, and things, but they will be in their perfect form. This statement is glorious and healing for us as we walk through grief. Our loved ones are restored. Our favorite places will be reestablished. The things we deeply love, miss, or long for here will be on the new earth in ways so much better than we ever could've imagined. I cannot wait for that day.

Grief Is Inconvenient (Melody) ✳

After going through something so painful and losing our son Kanaan, David and I knew we needed to do some grief counseling and processing together and separately. We realized we had not fully grieved our other losses because we were so focused on "fixing" what was wrong with our bodies. Grief is something I never thought I would have to deal with so much in our marriage and at the start of having a family. Before we had our first miscarriage, we did not know how common it can be to have

---

[5] "G3824 - Palingenesia - Strong's Greek Lexicon (Kjv)," Blue Letter Bible, accessed March 24, 2025, https://www.blueletterbible.org/lexicon/g3824/kjv/tr/0-1/.

[6] John Eldredge, All Things New: Heaven, Earth, and the Restoration of Everything You Love (Thomas Nelson, 2017).

a miscarriage or lose a child. These are the things that no one likes to talk about and ruin the joy of a young married couple. The reality is our world and bodies are imperfect, and there will always be loss and death until Jesus comes back and makes everything perfect like Him. God still heals every day, and He wants us to be in the best health, but the enemy and sin are still at play to try and influence all areas of our lives.

Each person responds to loss differently. You can choose to lean into God or blame Him and walk away. Mourning can lead you to comfort or unbelief. We see this in Scripture: "When Jesus rose early on the first day of the week, he appeared first to Mary Magdalene, out of whom he had driven seven demons. She went and told those who had been with him and who were mourning and weeping. When they heard that Jesus was alive and that she had seen him, they did not believe it" (Mark 16:9–11).

Mourning kept these people from believing.

David and I chose to press into our faith, but we also had many questions. I remember times when grief would come out of nowhere and hit me like a train. I remember being at a concert with some ladies while our guys were gone hunting. It was a fun, upbeat concert by an artist I liked. One song in particular just hit me, and I didn't feel like being there anymore. I lost interest in the rest of the concert and couldn't stop thinking about our son. Grief does that. It comes inconveniently into your life. It's necessary for the healing journey, but it tests you. Your emotions can seem out of control even though your mind knows the truth.

I realized early on that triggers for me were a real thing. I had to be careful and say no to many things surrounding babies and very young children for a time because it was all so fresh and painful. For me, it was a constant reminder until I could process it and learn to live with my losses. I remember attending a kid's birthday party the day after Kanaan's funeral. If I could go back in time, I would have told myself, "Give yourself grace; people will understand if you don't go, and if they do not understand, they simply do not have to live with the reality you are living." That was probably the most emotionally challenging birthday party I ever went to. We had officially put our son in the ground the day prior, and I needed to put a smile on my face for a celebration the next day. Grief makes you befriend your emotions. It makes you fully embrace what you are experiencing and uncovers what you believe in your heart.

The days following loss are complex and feel as if they will stretch on forever. But you get through it and even learn to grow around it. You learn to enjoy life again once you have allowed yourself to process how you are feeling and where you are with everything. Grief changes you. It changes the lens through which you see experiences in your specific season. Generally, we choose what an experience or event means for us, either positive or negative. Tragic loss is an exception. It never comes at a good time, and nothing is ever good about it, but good can come from it. God will use it for good, but that doesn't mean what happened was good.

Grief Moves Us Forward (Melody)

Fall is my favorite time of year. Seeing the colors on the trees signals the coming of a different season. I love walking in the red, orange, and yellow-hued leaves as I take a deep breath of fresh air. Grief changes in seasons, just like the colors of the autumn leaves. Each stage and season brings a different aspect of grief. It doesn't leave forever, gone into the abyss. It doesn't even necessarily change in size or shrink. Grief stays while you learn to live your life around it. The saying that "time heals" is not reality. Time doesn't make your grief disappear. But it does give you the tools to keep moving forward. You end up building experiences around it. As you process and put action into your grief, you add another layer around it as you live your life.

Grief makes us process the things we go through. It's a natural response to the absence of what we cherish. It makes you stop, even momentarily, to absorb your feelings. Take a moment right now to pause and honor the hard you have experienced.

Grief helps us push through another day. It's the gray mixed into our life's color palate. It changes from one moment to the next, never the same. Grief is like a body ache—we learn to live with it, but that doesn't mean we wallow in sadness forever. Without grief, we are barely human. Our lives are not perfect, so for every one of us, there is something that we grieve. It means you encountered a significant loss because you loved a person deeply. It honors the memories and emotions attached to it. The only way for us to live is to embrace grief. Grief exists where love lived first. *Grief hurts so much because you love so deeply.*

Learning to live with grief takes you through a series of stages. These stages do not necessarily come in order in your journey. The five stages of grief include denial, anger, bargaining, depression, and acceptance. For us, it was a roller coaster going back and forth between the stages. There were many times when I thought I was ready to return to normalcy and everyday life. I remember attending a women's conference just a month after Kanaan passed. I realized that it was not a good decision for me to go. I pushed past what I felt but walked away from it even more heartbroken because it was not the right timing for me in that season. I was just not ready.

I want you to know that if you are grieving right now, give yourself plenty of grace and space. They go hand in hand—the grace to say no or yes to things and the space to let yourself feel the feelings and let them out. Feelings are not interruptions; they are invitations to let God in. Grief is an invitation to heal and grow deeper. We must embrace our circumstances, engage our emotions, endure the process, and enjoy the healing effects. Most of the time, healing comes in the process.

Grief in Community (Melody)

Have you ever felt like you had to stuff your emotions? Events happen in our lives that we cannot control, but we can control our beliefs and the consequent emotions that come from them. Whatever we believe influences how we react.

The truth is that our emotions should be a gauge, not a guide. We can't deny them, but they shouldn't constantly direct us. Determine the facts about your situation, your beliefs about it, and your feelings. Beliefs are not always facts; they are feelings of certainty. Our feelings will follow what we focus on. We need to learn to file our feelings properly once we feel them and then let them go. If we leave them unprocessed, they will come up later in life, often more intensely.

For me, there was deep sorrow and even depression at times. People got awkward around me. They didn't know what to say or how to react when they saw me. It was hard for both David and me. Some would acknowledge it, and some wouldn't at all. People not recognizing what I had just been through was hurtful. It felt like they were too embarrassed or scared to say something wrong, so instead, they said nothing. Acknowledging my son was so important to me, and it hurt when others did not. Grief visits everyone who has lost a loved one, and people become overly uncomfortable. They go to great lengths to avoid acknowledging or talking about it. Grieving people end up feeling lonely, isolated, and unsupported. This is why unrecognized pain turns into external and internal destructive behaviors. In this case, grieving people do not know that what they are experiencing is normal. This all improves when grief is talked about and the experience is normalized.

Unfortunately, our country does not do grief well. No one likes to talk about it because it's uncomfortable. We hope grief leaves us alone, and we go on pretending it does not exist. That is not how sorrow works. Some grief therapists even tend to induce shame when people experiencing grief do not "get over it" or "recover" fast enough. People get too intolerant of those walking through grief and chalk that up as something they can't handle, so they run away from situations like that.

As believers watching someone grieve, we need to learn to listen and sit with people. On the other hand, we also must be able to celebrate with others who are celebrating. The Bible says, "Rejoice with those who rejoice; mourn with those who mourn" (Rom. 12:15). However, the expectation that grieving believers should be able to rejoice with those who are rejoicing does not consider where those people are in their grieving. When done too soon, it can make that grieving person resentful toward the one celebrating, or it can keep the person mourning from actively moving forward in their grief. Everyone is at different stages in their grief, and some can do that, but others cannot. One day, they will be able to!

Jesus modeled both grieving and rejoicing; He would grieve with someone one day and rejoice with another the next. Grief makes us human, and like Jesus, we also weep. Of course, Jesus grieved perfectly; He never let His grief overwhelm Him, and it never led Him to step out of sync with the Father. I never want grief to take me away from God or the people in my life who love me. Even in our brokenness, we can yield to God.

Grief done in a healthy way should lead you to a closer relationship with Christ and bring human relationships to a deeper level. It won't happen with everyone, and you might naturally distance or grow away from others who are just not meant to be in your inner circle anymore. You will learn to see who truly cares about you and your situation. On the other hand, as the griever, you sometimes have to let people know what you need. You can't expect them to understand what you need because they can't read your mind. You might not even know what you need in your grief journey. It might be hard to accept things or ask for things. Either way, grace must be given in all directions. Grief doesn't involve just losing someone to death. It can be from losing a job or relationship you hoped for. It can come from any painful experience you have had. It's emotionally, mentally, and physically tiring and trying. It's a time when you need support around you, whatever that looks like.

Not many people in my life understood what I was going through or were willing to talk about it. I had to lean into other support systems. Some of the specific resources I found helpful were one-on-one counseling, the Missing GRACE Foundation, Hope Mommies, the Joyful Mourning community, and Waiting for Baby Bird Ministries. Now that more time has passed, I do not need all these resources as much, but on specific holidays or milestones, I know I can find support when needed. Knowing that I am and was not alone in this experience has been helpful. No two stories or experiences are the same. Each family is unique, and there will be different levels of difficulty in your story. There will also be various levels of good! Grief can seem like a mountain you must climb that you are not ready for. You need help and support along the way. You may need to take breaks and refresh yourself (self-care) on the way up. You never think you can make it, but with each baby step, you eventually do! You do not get there in one day, but with many days of processing, strategizing, grieving, and healing, you will.

Grief Takes a Toll (Melody) ✶ ─────────────────────

The changes in my physical body involved a different kind of grief process. After giving birth to my son, I grieved with all the reminders in my body from having a baby. There are things that people do not think about, such as your milk still coming in, healing from birth, the mental and emotional trauma, and more. It was a struggle to get up every day and to do the simple things like getting dressed, brushing my teeth, eating, and doing anything productive.

I planned to be a stay-at-home mom, so I wasn't working anymore except trying to put time into my wellness business while doing school online. I didn't have somewhere I went every day to connect with people. I didn't have a specific time to be up and out the door. I didn't have anyone expecting me to get a certain amount of work done. I was at home, alone, trying to survive. For almost an entire year, I didn't have much of an appetite. I lost many pounds of weight and got extremely skinny. My hormones and thyroid were all messed up, and I had to go on thyroid medication just to help me through. All the natural stuff I was doing was just not enough because my emotional and mental stress was so high. My body suffered.

My spiritual life also struggled. I was trying to grieve in the best way I knew, but this was my first time going through a loss like this and all the trauma attached to it, as well as postpartum depression. (We will talk about trauma in a later chapter). I went into a deep, dark hole of despair for a time. It was hard to look at things in a positive light. My dreams felt stolen and crushed forever. Grieving all the firsts Kanaan would have had was devastating—his first cry, laugh, smile, being held by his grandpa and grandma, his first hunting trip with Dad, his first milestones, and his first birthday. We had already filled our minds with future memories, and now, we would never get to see him in those moments. Every time we saw our parents smile joyfully with one of the other grandkids, it was hard because we knew Kanaan was missing out on that. Kanaan left us too soon.

It was as though I could not get out of this hole. I remember that I did not even want to read my Bible for a time. I tried to hold onto the words in Scripture and the promises God had spoken to us, but they seemed invalid. The complete opposite had just happened in our lives. How could this be? Why did we lose this child?

In the midst of this, I remembered that God, too, lost His son. Jesus was perfectly loved by God. He was His only son. God gave Him as a sacrifice for all of us so that we could all be in God's kingdom. I can't imagine willingly giving up my son. With all the plans, hopes, and dreams a parent has for their child, that would feel like the most tremendous loss and sacrifice of their life. But God did it. He knew it would bring not just one but many people like us to a place where we could have salvation and be part of His family forever.

Where Will Grief Take You? (Melody) ✳━━━━━━━━━

God knew we would feel this way. He knew these things would happen, yet He didn't cause it. You might say, "He didn't stop it when He could have, though." That is true, but one thing we can't control is the sin in the world. Because the enemy is still roaming around, ready to steal, kill, and destroy, bad things still happen. One day, God will recover it all!

Until then, we wrestle with how to live on this earth knowing that God has already won the victory, but we must choose to walk in it every day until the very end. This is the hope I had to learn to hold onto—a hope that I would see my babies again one day in glory with God. I knew that because of God's promise, He would one day make all things new. All the pain and heartache you have gone through will be turned upside down in eternity.

While we're waiting for that day, we long for fulfillment here and now. When you are in pain or heartache, you need constant nourishment; it helps you embrace the most difficult situations in your life. God prepares a table for us in the presence of our enemies (Ps. 23:5). This table brings nourishment and fellowship with the Father. But in these painful moments, we struggle to find the table. We become preoccupied and think we will use spiritual warfare to escape or fight, but sometimes, relief comes from rest and surrender. Your grief season is like a manna season (see Exodus 16). You have enough in God today, and He will give you enough when tomorrow comes.

Our goal should be to want the comfort that welcomes the presence of God. We find this by pouring into the scriptures. Psalm 25 is an excellent place to start. "My hope is in you all day long" (Ps. 25:5). Give God an offering of surrender. Acknowledge Him in your pain. That offering, in the middle of pain, starts a journey. He wants to hear us say how we feel. God knows us perfectly, but He will work so much more freely when we have opened ourselves up. We must come to Him wholly exposed, hiding nothing because He already knows.

So, will your mourning take you to unbelief or to the comforter? Are you mourning in HOPE? If you maintain hope when things look hopeless or you can't explain why something happened, it enables you to go into weeping. You retain the hope and welcome the comforter, God. There are measures of God's character that can only be found in the darkest valley of death. *That is where God reveals His most incredible peace and comfort to us.*

"To receive the peace that surpasses understanding, you have to give up your right to understand."[7] Bill Johnson repeatedly says this phrase, and after Kanaan's death, I finally understood it. Giving up your right to understand doesn't mean you won't ever understand what happened and why; it does mean first things first. Give it to God. If you don't give up that right, you are still holding onto control of your situation. It's hard and not fun, but receiving God's lasting peace is necessary. There is a chance you might never understand until you get to Heaven, but that's part of living in mystery with God. When we misapply understanding, we don't have peace. When the questions come, it's easy to go toward unbelief. When you can lay down understanding and receive peace, the questions won't drive you to unbelief. The questions will come, but they won't break your foundation in God.

Some of the best advice I have is not to avoid grief or mourning. Give God something to work with. Everything short of surrender gives us problems. Great faith comes from great surrender. It's like signing your name at the bottom of the contract before God fills in the details!

Sometimes, it hurts so much, and we do not understand why we still have empty arms, but someday we will have full arms. God is so good no matter what our circumstances look like. He didn't cause them, but He walks with us through them. His redemption, promises, and breakthroughs will come. I will always have hope. I can't not have it! It's not an option for us. If we do not have hope in Him, there is nothing to live for.

[7] Bill Johnson.
https://www.facebook.com/photo
php?fbid=1078386580321200&id=100044496036943&set=a.260691375424062.

Reflection:

~ Has your grief or trial led you to hope or despair?

Prayer:

Lord, I need You in the middle of my grief. I ask You to show up in ways that bring healing and comfort right now. Be my counselor, friend, and comfort. Walk with me through this pain. Help me to get through it with Your help and grace. In Jesus's name, I pray. Amen.

Chapter 4
GRAVES TO GARDENS

The Spirit of the Lord God is upon me,

Because the Lord has anointed me

To bring good news to the humble;

He has sent me to bind up the brokenhearted,

To proclaim release to captives

And freedom to prisoners;

To proclaim the favorable year of the Lord

And the day of vengeance of our God;

To comfort all who mourn,

To grant those who mourn in Zion,

Giving them a garland instead of ashes,

The oil of gladness instead of mourning,

The cloak of praise instead of a disheartened spirit.

So they will be called oaks of righteousness,

The planting of the Lord, that He may be glorified.

—Isaiah 61:1–3 NASB

Faith sees the light in your heart when your eyes see darkness ahead. As we surrendered and gave what little we had to God, He was gracious to give us glimpses of joy and peace in the middle of the sadness. One of those glimpses came from none other than our son's funeral.

A Beautiful Life (Melody) ✶ ———————————————

On a beautiful fall day, September 24, 2021, Kanaan Asher's funeral occurred at our church. Our families, friends, coworkers, and church friends were there. About 150 people came for a baby boy they did not even know. It was a day we did not want to come, but we had to put his little body to rest. As I walked up to the vessel that held his tiny body, topped with the baby blue shoes I had picked out for him during my pregnancy, I lost it. It hit me. We were at a funeral service for our son. It's something no parent should ever have to do. We sang about the goodness of God and the hope of Heaven. Little did we know what an impact our son would have that day. David shared a special letter he wrote about what Kanaan experienced while on earth; it reminded us of all the good and precious moments we had with him. I want to share a piece of that letter here:

✶ I came into existence when God Himself spoke me into being in January 2021. Mommy and Daddy were so happy to hear about my life and my soon-to-be arrival. I got to see them cry happy tears and shout for joy. I felt so loved by them and by Jesus from day one.

Like most firstborn sons, my life was already planned out for me. Daddy was dreaming of me being a three-sport athlete and sharing in his hunting adventures. Mommy was busy getting the nursery ready. She was dreaming of all the sweet cuddles we would share and all the milestones I would accomplish! Both Mommy and Daddy were excited to introduce me to my Lord and Savior, Jesus, and they were praying and learning every day how to raise me right.

I got to see the sheer joy in both my grandmas and grandpas when they first heard of me. Early in my life, we celebrated Mommy's twenty-seventh birthday. The month after that, I got to experience Kimball High School's first state championship in wrestling. My daddy is the head coach. I was so proud and excited to wrestle someday!

Soon after that, I got on my first airplane, and I went with Mommy and Daddy to Florida! They both graduated from the Wellness Way Academy, and they were so excited to help people in their health journeys! We also hung out at the beach. It was so fun and beautiful! I loved collecting seashells with Mom and Dad and seeing the historic city of St. Augustine!

After we got home from the trip, I started moving a lot in Mommy's belly. I remember Daddy feeling my punches and kicks for the first time! He was so proud of me, and I started doing more and more tricks! I remember Mommy and Daddy reading me stories at night. My favorites were the stories about Noah's ark and all the animals, as well as when David (my daddy's name) defeated the big giant. I loved being a part of prayer times and taking communion with Mommy and Daddy.

I then got to be a part of a very special day! Auntie Bailey and Uncle Logan got married in the preserve's pine forest! It was one of my favorite memories because it was so pretty. I love all my uncles and aunties and cousins very much. It was extra special because I got to be part of the ceremony in front of all my loved ones! You can see me in all the pictures! Daddy even did the wedding ceremony! Many people told him it was one of the most beautiful weddings they ever saw. I'd have to agree.

After that, I went on one more trip with Mommy and Daddy to Door County, Wisconsin. I loved kayaking in Lake Michigan and watching the beautiful sunsets. I even indulged in some excellent goat milk ice cream! It was so yummy. When we got home, I remember being able to watch some preseason Vikings games with Daddy. They were so fun! Daddy told me he would bring me to one someday. One of my favorite things was being in nature at the preserve. Mommy and Daddy took me on daily walks as we prayed and worshipped Jesus. I got to help Mommy and Daddy prepare for hunting season! I got so excited when I helped Daddy put the cameras in the right spots and when I got to shoot bows with my mom and dad. We saw some beautiful animals, but let me tell you, they are nothing compared to what I get to watch every day with my brother and sister!

I got to be a part of a shower where I got many gifts! I was excited to play with them! Soon after, I remember Jesus asking me if I would stay with Him. I didn't know what to say, and my mommy, daddy, grandparents, uncles, aunts, and cousins were upset. They cried and cried. They wanted me to stay with them longer, and I didn't want to see them that way. I told Jesus to comfort them and give them peace. He told me that He gave them His Holy Spirit to be with them and help them. September 7, 2021, was my birthday. I weighed three pounds and was fifteen inches long. I had a perfect mix of Mommy and Daddy's hair. Jesus took me to my forever home that day. If you are hearing this, it is so much better than you could imagine! The beauty, the hunting, the sports, and the food are so much better than anything I experienced on earth! I love being with Jesus all of the time. We sing my favorite songs to Him right alongside angels and heroes that Mommy and Daddy told me about! I love being with my brother, sister, and five cousins here in Heaven! We are so excited to welcome you all in just a short time! I love you!

Kanaan impacted many people who gave their hearts to God on the day of his funeral. We will never forget those who raised their hands to enter into a relationship with the one true God. It was a decision that would change their lives forever. The Lord so kindly helped us get through the service and covered us with His peace. The greater the sorrow, the sweeter the grace of Jesus.

After the service, our families and a couple of close friends came with us to a piece of our family property. This land would now become "The Land of Kanaan." There, David and I had stood almost seven years earlier saying, "I do," to the rest of our lives. Now, we were making a memorial area for our son in the same place. We planted a tree as a reminder that our love for Kanaan and our longing for Heaven would continue to grow. As our families stood around, we prayed that God would heal our hearts and fill us with peace. We didn't ask for answers. We didn't ask for the pain to leave. We did ask for God to come close to our severely aching hearts. The Lord was beginning to give us a crown of beauty as His son and daughter instead of ashes. We gave our son's ashes to God, and He gave us His healing oil. We decided that day that this piece of land would become a garden of healing—from a grave to a garden and from bitter to sweet. Every loss would become a seed that would later bring life.

The following days and weeks changed significantly. Everyone, including family, returned to their everyday lives, but our world had stopped. It was like being stuck in an elevator but never being able to get out and get on a different floor. Our son was gone, and there was nothing we could do to change that. We could only hope for the day that we would see him and be together again.

God's Unchanging Character (Melody) ✳━━━━━━━━

As I was reading the book of Habakkuk, I was reminded of God being faithful to His covenant. In Habakkuk, God's people were judged and taken captive by the Babylonians. So many evil and bad things were happening to God's chosen people. Habakkuk knew who the Lord was, but the character of God didn't seem to match the situation in front of his eyes. We must understand this: At some point in our lives, we will need to reconcile our theology and experience. We will have to wrestle with the evil in the world when we serve a good God. When we don't understand where God is or what He is doing, we will be tempted to change our theology to align with what is happening in the world or our situation. We must stand on the truth of the Word of God and His goodness. We trusted that God was working in ways that we could not see. We trusted that He was good. We knew that God didn't cause this to happen to us. We knew that He never created sickness or disease. He is a good God.

Habakkuk wasn't afraid to cry out to God. "God, how long do I have to cry out for help before you listen? How many times do I have to yell, 'Help! Murder! Police!' before you come to the rescue? Why do you force me to look at evil, stare trouble in the face day after day?" (Hab. 1:2–3 MSG). As Habakkuk lamented, so we lamented in the season we were in. Habakkuk understood that he could lament to God. However, he did not allow his sorrow or the despair of the Israelites to change how he viewed God's goodness. God's character does not change. We ought to be reminded that life can be messy, painful, joyful, and filled with grief and laughter simultaneously. Don't try to plot it on a straight path because you will lose every time! God will use our darkest days to bring light into someone else's world.

Putting Grief into Action (Melody) ✳━━━━━━━━━━━━━

As we mourned with God, He gave us peace that surpassed our understanding, but only because we gave up our right to understand. He wants to provide His peace for us! God also revealed various ways we could put our grief into action during this time. We started to add flowers and symbolic decor to the Land of Kanaan. Bees represented all three of our children in Heaven. They were all a part of our hive, and we believed

God was making sweet, healing honey from them. Bees became my symbol for Kanaan because he represented the promised land where milk and honey were found in the Bible. Tending to the garden and his memorial helped us feel like we were taking care of him. It was one of the few things I could do to mother my children in Heaven.

Out of our pain, we ministered to other grieving parents like us as we created and sent out "hope boxes" to moms and dads who needed to know that someone could understand what they were going through. We shared our testimony of Kanaan and hosted a Christmas decorating event the following year with our friend Candy from the Missing GRACE Foundation to help families honor their babies in Heaven. We connected with a grief group, and I joined a grieving moms' Bible study. It helped us gain support and share our story. It helped us know that what we felt was valid and that we were not alone. From that, we decided to write blog posts and create a social media page in honor of Kanaan called "The Land of Kanaan." There, we shared our grief, joy, hard days and good days, things the Lord put on our hearts, and encouragement for other parents and families experiencing loss.

A Glimpse of Heaven (Melody) ✳

As I pressed into the Lord one day, He gave me a beautiful picture of Heaven. I share it with you in hopes that it encourages you and gives you hope that you will see your children or other loved ones in Heaven restored and made whole. Let the Lord minister to you as you read this.

✳   A gentle breeze brushes over your face as you feel a warmth from the sun. You suddenly feel refreshed, and you open your eyes. You smile. You're not on vacation; you're in paradise. You hear laughs, singing, and conversations taking place. You step out of your room onto a big balcony over a green patch of grass—the most perfect green grass. The smells are vibrant. You realize all your senses are perfect. You smell the fresh fruit hanging off trees below you and see kids laughing and playing and others engaging in a way you never thought possible.

You make your way down the stairs and out the front door and are greeted with the biggest hug! It's your child, the one you have been waiting to see for so long. The only emotion you feel is complete joy and peace. No tears stream down your face. No past pain is felt. You realize you are in Heaven with your beloved child or children you never met or got to know on earth. You pick them up and spin them around. It feels as though you have endless time with them. Time moves at a much different pace than when you were on the earth. You waste no time packing a picnic and heading to your child's favorite place, the one they have been waiting to show you!

You spend the whole day there with them, soaking in all the memories made, not because there isn't time but because you are enjoying every minute of it. You've waited so long for these moments. Walking back home with your family, you realize God was watching the joy that filled your heart. He was even more excited than you were, knowing He would also get to enjoy those moments of being reunited. The days your heart yearned for are finally here. You're in Heaven enjoying everything you were made for, especially those you love so deeply. You're so glad you yearned for Heaven and kept hoping you would be reunited again one day. "He will wipe every tear from their eyes, and there will be no more death or sorrow or crying or pain. All these things are gone forever" (Rev. 21:4 NLT).

I was in tears. The vision God gave me in that moment gave me immense peace. I knew that He could be trusted—that He was caring for my children in the best way possible. At that moment, I was reminded of this passage:

✴ If God hadn't been there for me,
I never would have made it.
The minute I said, "I'm slipping, I'm falling,"
your love, God, took hold and held me fast.
When I was upset and beside myself,
you calmed me down and cheered me up. (Ps. 94:17–19 MSG)

These verses showed me that He was speaking to me, calming my spirit, and bringing me peace and joy. I became so interested in Heaven because I had not just one but three precious children there. Answers would not fix my aching heart; only God's presence and peace would. What could I offer Him amid a life-changing moment? Worship. Worshiping in pain is only possible on this side of Heaven, so it is both a sacrifice and a privilege. Sometimes, giving God worship is easy and enjoyable, but there are days that it costs me. Grab your "moment," whether good or bad and give an offering to God!

Through the Mire (Melody) ✴━━━━━━━━━━━━━━━━

Psalm 40:2–3 says, "He lifted me out of the pit of despair, out of the mud and the mire. He set my feet on solid ground and steadied me as I walked along. He has given me a new song to sing, a hymn of praise to our God. Many will see what he has done and be amazed. They will put their trust in the Lord."

✴ I love what Matthew Henry's Bible commentary says about these verses:

The psalmist waited patiently; he continued believing, hoping, and praying. This is applicable to Christ. His agony, in the garden and on the cross, was a horrible pit and miry clay. But those that wait patiently for God do not wait in vain. Those that have been under religious melancholy, and by the grace of God have been relieved, may apply ver. (2) very feelingly to themselves; they are brought up out of a horrible pit. Christ is the Rock on which a poor soul can alone stand fast. Where God has given stedfast hope, he expects there should be a steady, regular walk and conduct. God filled the psalmist with joy, as well as peace in believing.[8]

Going through grief feels like a mire. What is a mire? A mire is an area of wet, spongy earth, like a bog or marsh.[9] In this psalm, David says he is stuck in a challenging place, and it seems there is no escape. But David decides to grab his moment and give an offering of praise to God.

When we walk with God, we sometimes have trials that seem to continue. There can appear to be no hope of them ever ending. These miry bogs result from uncompromisable waves of hardship in life. We constantly have to keep getting up from each punch.

On his own, David was powerless to escape. The only thing he could do was wait patiently for the Lord to rescue him. Waiting on God is not easy. We never know God's timeline, but we develop endurance and perseverance while waiting. God lifted David out of despair. He was set on solid ground and secured. He was given a new song to sing. Sometimes, blessings cannot be received unless we go through the trial of waiting. Waiting on God does not mean sitting back and doing nothing. Instead,

[8]

Chapter Four

Matthew Henry and Thomas Scott, *Matthew Henry's Consise Commentary* (Oak Harbor, WA: Logos Research Systems, 1997), Ps 40:1

[9] "Mire," Merriam-Webster, accessed February 4, 2025, https://www.merriam-webster.com dictionary/mire.

waiting involves examining our lives. We need to see if anything needs to be acknowledged or left behind. Waiting includes putting our attention to the things of God. Tend to the gardens He is growing in you. Praise Him in the good days and hard days, the hurt and the joy. Let your praise to Him bring you up out of the pit. Let your "moments" be a sacrifice of praise.

Reflection:

~   What are some moments that you can still choose to give God praise in?

Prayer:

Lord, show me how You are making my ashes into beauty. Fill me with hope for eternity. Be with me as I navigate this season and receive Your truth in love. Make my ashes into beauty this year. In Jesus's name, I pray. Amen.

Chapter 5

GOD'S GOODNESS IS NOURISHMENT FOR THE JOURNEY

But you are not like that, for you are a chosen people. You are royal priests, a holy nation, God's very own possession. As a result, you can show others the goodness of God, for he called you out of the darkness into his wonderful light.

— 1 Peter 2:9 NLT

Jesus always has a redemptive solution. You are chosen; you are loved. You are a recipient of God's goodness! You might ask how moments of grief and trials in life represent that God is still good. Are you willing to live with some mystery in your journey with God? In life?

Release His Goodness (Melody)

What does the goodness of God mean? It is grace. It is mercy. It is redemption. It is all that and more. It is His perfect plan. It is His perfect character. One Bible dictionary puts it this way:

* A perfection of his character which he exercises towards his creatures according to their various circumstances and relations (Ps. 145:8, 9; 103:8; 1 John 4:8). Viewed generally, it is benevolence; as exercised with respect to the miseries of his creatures it is mercy, pity, compassion, and in the case of impenitent sinners, long-suffering patience; as exercised in communicating favour on the unworthy it is grace. "Goodness and justice are the several aspects of one unchangeable, infinitely wise, and sovereign moral perfection. God is not sometimes merciful and sometimes just, but he is eternally infinitely just and merciful." God is infinitely and unchangeably good (Zeph. 3:17), and his goodness is incomprehensible by the finite mind (Rom. 11:35, 36). "God's goodness appears in two things, giving and forgiving."[10]

We can have hope when we believe that God is good. When we wear this lens of God's goodness, we see God for who He truly is. When this is at the core of our theology, it determines how we do life and who we are. It shapes our demeanor and affirms that despite what happens in our lives, God will use it for His glory. It helps us stop asking "why" about everything and brings us to a spot where we can be a part of God's solution.

Your mystery moments (not understanding your circumstances) are even more valuable when looking at the goodness of God. You develop trust in God through them. You may not see tomorrow clearly, but you can

---

10

Chapter Five

M. G. Easton, *Illustrated Bible Dictionary and Treasury of Biblical History, Biography, Geography, Doctrine, and Literature* (New York: Harper & Brothers, 1893), 296.

hang on and trust God for the things that are unseen right now that He has promised. He will give us what we need for our next set of circumstances! He will remain a good Father through it all. We have the blessing of representing His goodness in our lives. When we can bring this discovery of God's heart in a palpable way, people will experience the Lord's goodness. Our words release what we are most aware of. So, if we are aware of God's goodness, we will release His goodness in our lives by what we speak. I remember many times when God revealed His goodness to me through His comfort, love, and faithfulness, and He brought about deeper meaning and growth through our pain.

God Is for You (David)

I love the story of Samson in Judges for so many reasons. I think it's a clear picture of how God uses imperfect people and challenging situations to show up and show off like He does time and time again. The whole story is worth a read, but in summary, like our story, it starts with a battle with infertility.

Side note: I think it's astounding that so many of our modern chronic diseases have been man-made. It's been because of industrialization, diet, lifestyle, etc., but infertility seems to be a battle as old as time. There are physical components, as we've learned, but I think the battle is more of a spiritual one. Regardless, if we remain humble and continue to cry out to God, He always shows up. He does it repeatedly, and the result is usually children who are marked, called, and equipped to do mighty exploits for the kingdom of God! God loves children and the next generation. The enemy hates these. God always wins! I love that.

Back to the story: Monoah and his wife are barren. An angel of God shows up to Monoah's wife and tells her that she will conceive and give birth to a son. He tells her to abstain from alcohol and any unclean food. She then runs to tell her husband, and he cries out for the same encounter! (You can read the story in Judges 13). I love this because it shows his humanity. It's not a story of a mighty man of faith. He had doubts, just like many of us do when we hear a promise or hear God speak. He asks for the angel to visit again. In the kindness of our Father, the angel does come back but again only appears to Monoah's wife! The angel is so patient and kind that he allows her time to run and get her husband!

To make a long story short, they get confirmation, they obey, and the word God gave them comes to pass! It's Samson. He's another fantastic study. He's one of the most anointed people in the Bible, yet he's incredibly flawed. He lets lust get the best of him time and time again, which inevitably becomes his downfall, but because of God's grace, Samson is used to lead great conquests of the Philistines for Israel! God is so good that He even uses Samsons lusts and desires to bring Him glory and benefit the nation of Israel.

If you read the story, it all starts because he has the hots for a Philistine woman. That was a no-no that nobody approved of. Israelites weren't supposed to marry the Philistines, but Samson saw what he wanted and went after her despite his parents' disapproval. He was going to marry her, and he went on a trip to see her. On the way, he encountered a lion, and the Bible says in Judges 14:6 (TPT), "The Spirit of Yahweh entered Samson and empowered him to tear the lion to pieces with his bare hands."

This is incredible. The whole story is only a few Bible verses, and Samson chooses not to tell people about it. Get this: On his way to doing something against his parent's will, the Spirit of God empowers him to rip apart a lion with his hands! If we are being honest, most of us would turn back at the first sight of a lion. One of the most admirable qualities I think Samson exudes is that he was absolutely convinced God was for him—no matter what. He had a revelation of the goodness and the friendship of God that would change our lives. It gets even better. Fast forward, and Samson is making a second trip to see the Philistine woman. On his way, he saw the lion's carcass with bees and honey in it. He grabbed some and ate on his journey. Touching the carcass of the dead lion was in violation of his vow to

God, but even so, God provides nourishment for the journey from his past battles and victories.

I've seen this in our journey too. Our past victories nourish us for the journey. We never necessarily arrive, but we continue to feast on the testimonies and every word that God speaks (Matt. 4:4). Let this story encourage you that no matter what you've done, God is for you when you cry out to Him. He uses all of it. Nothing is wasted.

Do I Believe God Is Good? (David) ✳——————————

Our God is an awesome God. The Bible says that we serve the same God today that Abraham, Isaac, and Jacob served. The same God who parted seas, rescued people from lions and giants, provided manna from the sky, and even raised people from the dead is the God who we, as Christ followers, get to have a personal and intimate relationship with. He speaks to us through His written Word, His Holy Spirit, creation, music, experiences, and so many other ways. God is infinite. He's all-powerful, He's all-knowing, and He's sovereign. He still heals, He still speaks, and He still creates. It's incredible that He chooses to co-labor with us, partner with us, and do mighty things in and through us! We will never fully comprehend His deep, unfailing, unending love for us until we lock eyes with Him one day. Even this description of Him seems like a gross understatement, but our English language has limits. Our God is good!

We hear these things, read these things, and experience these things. We believe them as we grow up in the church, get exposed to His Word, and start seeing His miraculous power at work. We believe it, ultimately, because it's 100 percent true. But while we believe all of this, is it okay if I'm human for a second? May I be honest, authentic, and raw? There are times that the words written above don't feel true. They seem to contradict themselves. They may be true at times, but not all the time. They may be true for others, but not for me.

I remember sitting next to Melody, holding our son, Kanaan.

Instead of the usual baby cries, we were crying uncontrollably, just hoping the tears falling on our dead son's face would bring him back to life. His chromosomal abnormalities shaped his tiny body and face in ways that weren't natural. It felt like a nightmare, but I knew it wasn't. Everything had escalated and moved so fast that we were still in shock. Fast forward a few weeks, and I found myself breaking ground with a shovel. The last time I dug a hole in this ground was during our beautiful wedding ceremony, but this time, it was to bury my firstborn son. The son that I believed God promised and would protect was dead. He wasn't sick or in the NICU or even needing a lot of special care. He was dead. There was nothing we could do. Burying Kanaan was more than burying my son. It was burying my future, my hope, my dreams, and even my trust and faith in God.

How could a good God allow this? Nothing was good about it, and it didn't make any sense. It was just pain, doubt, confusion, depression, and, quite frankly, lots of thoughts that I'd rather be in Heaven than here. I had dreamed about being a dad for so long. This felt like burying my dreams. I was so disappointed in God. He promised this and provided so much hope and encouragement during the journey. Even when we got the worst news ever about Kanaan's Trisomy 13, God brought a family to us that had a child who was supernaturally healed of a similar condition. It's hard to believe this now, but at the time, we were confident God would come through in the same way! Kanaan's story was too profound to end like this. I was disappointed because I thought God would come through, but He didn't. It felt like He forgot about us and the words He spoke. I honestly didn't know where to turn. I'd always turned to God and family in life's most challenging times, but this was different. They all felt distant because they couldn't possibly understand. Most people around us feared saying the wrong thing, so they resorted to saying nothing. It left us isolated in this season. We only had each other! We were two broken and undone people who needed any form of comfort possible.

Praising with Our Pain (David) ✱ ━━━━━━━━━━━━━━━

Looking back, I realize this was a significant crossroads in our life and story. We had a choice to make. If you're in the midst of this moment right now, as hard as it may seem, you have a clear choice to make. Were we going to keep going down this road with our God, whom we had come to know and love so deeply, or was this pain simply too much to overcome? Could He be trusted to fulfill what He said, or was that just for others or other times?

We thought we knew that God was a good God. We sing about it, read about it, and hear about it all the time, but how do we reconcile this with tragedy? We knew in our hearts that God did not cause this pain. He didn't make our son sick or kill him. However, we believe that He could have stopped it. He could have turned it around like He did for the family I mentioned earlier! That would have been some testimony. Maybe we would've already written books and birthed ministries out of that miracle. However, for reasons I still don't completely understand, God did not intervene like we had asked and thought He would.

The more I reflect, the more I realize how significant this crossroads is for you and was for us. When it was happening, we did not have much time to process or think about it like we do now. We looked at each other in our desperation and started saying things that we knew were true but that we didn't feel. We were praising in the middle of the storm and waiting for our souls to catch up with our words. God is so merciful and gracious. Even when I was considering being done with this thing called faith, He was there. Even when I was questioning Him, doubting Him, and losing my trust in Him, He was sitting right there! The Holy Spirit is our helper and comforter, and He showed up in the middle of our extreme lack of faith and reminded us of the truth.

Friends, understand this: When we get to Heaven and the restoration of all things, praise will be so natural and easy. We will be on the streets of gold with our children and the family of God. We will see sights, smell smells, hear sounds, taste goodness, and feel peace in ways our human mind cannot even imagine. Our praise won't cost us a thing; it will just be who we are! I cannot wait for that day! This life on earth is so short in light of eternity. I know it doesn't feel that way, especially right now. I understand. You see, in eternity, praise will be so easy because we will have no pain, no lack, no confusion, no doubt, and no questions. At the restoration of all things, it will make sense!

The writer of Hebrews says it much better than I can: "For we have no city here on earth to be our permanent home, but we seek the city that is destined to come. So we no longer offer up a steady stream of blood sacrifices, but through Jesus, we will offer up to God a steady stream of praise sacrifices—these are 'the lambs' we offer from our lips that celebrate his name!" (Heb. 13:14 TPT). These verses are so rich! While we wait for our permanent home, we have the privilege of offering up a sacrifice of praise to God, and He loves it! It's a sweet, sweet aroma that so pleases Him!

Let's look at another passage of Scripture: "Sacrifice thank offerings to God, fulfill your vows to the Most High . . . Those who sacrifice thank offerings honor me, and to the blameless I will show my salvation" (Ps. 50:14, 23). Sometimes, in the new covenant, we don't understand how to offer sacrifices to the Lord. We know that the days of blood atonements are over because Jesus fulfilled that at the cross, but Scripture is clear (even in the New Testament) that we celebrate His name through praise and sacrifices!

Pastor Bill Johnson shares similar insights through his grief journey after losing his wife, Beni. He says it is an honor and a privilege to praise God in times of significant loss, pain, confusion, doubt, questioning, etc.[11] Why? It's because we only get to do that here on earth. God never promised us an easy life here, and when we go through these varying levels of pain, we get to praise Him even in the middle. I believe that it is the sweetest aroma

---

[11] Bill Johnson, Bethel, "Join Us LIVE | Bethel Church," July 17, 2022, https://www.youtube.com/watch?v=lbUZk98T0l0.

in Heaven. It is storing up treasures in Heaven when we praise in moments when our flesh doesn't feel like it. We can surrender to the Holy Spirit and let Him minister to us! It's a profound privilege we will never get again once we cross into Heaven! There will be countless benefits in Heaven, but one thing is true. We will never get to praise Him with pain. Right now, we get that opportunity.

On Earth as It Is in Heaven (David) ✶────────────

After burying Kanaan in the memorial garden, we offered God a sacrifice of praise, and we still do it to this day. I remember many times lying prostrate by my son's grave, crying out to the Lord for comfort and, in turn, praising Him, even though my flesh wanted to blame Him, doubt Him, and question Him. Those moments were some of the most beautiful encounters with my heavenly Father that I've ever had. He came in comfort and provided reassurance that my children were thriving in their heavenly mandates. In those times, if only for a moment, Heaven invaded earth. If only for a moment, I got a glimpse and a taste of what it means to see the line in the Lord's prayer manifest: "On earth as it is in heaven" (Matt. 6:10).

I cannot begin to express the feeling of being at your firstborn son's funeral. It is so unnatural and wrong. As hard as it is to lose a grandparent or a parent, that is the natural circle of life. (And it's never our intention to undermine other painful experiences.) It doesn't mean it doesn't hurt and that you can't apply all these elements to those experiences! It simply means losing a child felt like another level of cruelty.

I got to address the amazing number of people who attended Kanaan's funeral. I expressed thanks and gratitude for the support they were showing us at that time, and we got to address them with the beautiful "letter from Kanaan" shared in this book. There wasn't a dry eye in the building, especially mine, as I tried to stumble through what we imagined Kanaan might want to say to his family and friends. As sudden as his stillbirth loss felt, we realized through this that we created some fantastic memories with him while he was safe and comfortable in Melody's tummy.

We began to see the Lord work in us and through us. We started seeing the Holy Spirit move across the room and our sphere of influence. As we shared that day about the future restoration of all things, we saw multiple people come to know Jesus! I can't imagine what Kanaan felt as he watched this with Jesus. There he was, in his restored heavenly glory—in eternity! Kanaan watched eternities change while experiencing the very thing that we all will experience one day! What a flood of emotions he must've felt. He got enough of a taste of his daddy's Vikings fandom that I imagine him "hitting the griddy" with the angels as hands went up to receive Jesus!

In those moments, I started to realize how God was transforming this situation for good. Let me be clear: There was NOTHING good about losing our child. You can't find a silver lining in losing a child before you get to see them take their first breath. As a faithful optimist, I tried! Nothing was good about the situation, yet EVERYTHING is good about our God. Hurts like this are the result of living in a fallen world where sin still has influence. It's not that it was any one person's fault or any one sin that caused this tragedy. It's just that the whole of living in a fallen world is greater than the sum of the sins and choices we all make.

God's kingdom had already come when Jesus invaded earth, but it will not be fully realized until He comes again with the saints to restore all things. We live in that tension. That is what makes it so difficult! We have delegated authority to enforce God's will on earth; sometimes, it manifests in supernatural healing, prophecy, signs, wonders, and the like. Sometimes, we pray all the right things, do all the right things, and say all the right things, but (at least at this moment) we don't see the breakthrough, the healing, or the word come to pass. This tension is oh-so-real! Friends, we all have a choice in these moments, whether they happen to us or whether we watch them happen to others. It's easy to lose faith or change what we believe to fit our circumstances. I've seen it happen to many people, and I empathize with them. I understand the temptation because the hurt is so great, and the disappointment is so real. Will we change our theology to match our experience, or will we keep going after the heart of God so much that, eventually, our experience matches our theology?

I've seen, heard, and read about people who start off believing in the fullness of the gospel. They believe that God heals and speaks and delivers, but when a trial comes, they walk away from God completely, or they change their theology to a more cessationist view—a belief that some miraculous gifts that we see in Scripture have not continued into modern times. Maybe you've heard the claims. Things like: Healing isn't for today, or the works of the Spirit ceased after the apostles. They've changed their theology to match their experience. They've been hurt, and I understand. Maybe you are there right now. It's okay! I'm not trying to persuade any theological view here. I'm simply saying that if I let my mind and spirit drift in that direction, the fruit is hopelessness, depression, despair, and apathy.

We choose to believe that God is our healer and that He wants to heal! He wants to heal us. He wants to heal you. Babies were His idea from the beginning, and that hasn't changed because we've experienced great pain. I still believe we will have biological children with us on earth. I believe God is healing us completely. He's healing our spirit, soul, and bodies, and I pray that every day, we become more like Him in every way. We're becoming whole and more restored with every passing day that we soak in His presence. I have seen too much, friends, to let my heart and soul drift to unbelief, even though it is so real and tempting sometimes! God is good! I've seen tumors shrink, deaf ears open, broken ribs fuse back together, and multiple sclerosis healed. I've read about it in Scripture, heard about it worldwide, and seen it with my own two eyes, all done in the mighty name of Jesus, whom we serve! I've tasted Heaven on earth, and even though I don't have it for every meal like I want, I crave it and go after it with the Lord because we owe that to the world and, most of all, to our Savior!

Surrender in Worship (David) ✳ ────────────

One of the most outstanding examples of faith through trials in the Bible is Job. If you've heard of Job and gone through grief, you've probably identified with him on some level. Job was a godly and wealthy man. The Bible says:

✳ There was a man in the land of Uz whose name was Job; and that man was blameless, upright, fearing God and turning away from evil. Seven sons and three daughters were born to him. His possessions were seven thousand sheep, three thousand camels, five hundred yoke of oxen, five hundred female donkeys, and very many servants; and that man was the greatest of all the men of the east. (Job 1:1–3 NASB)

Let's pause for a moment here. What a remarkable man! This guy had it all. He had the children and all the inheritance to pass on. He was the greatest man in the east! He was incredibly wealthy by today's standards, but even more importantly, he was blameless, upright, and honored in God's sight. I imagine that although no human is perfect, he was about as close to it as you could be on this side of eternity! The book of Job is interesting and unique because it records a conversation between God and Satan:

✳ The Lord said to Satan, "From where do you come?" Satan answered the Lord and said, "From roaming about on the earth and walking around on it." The Lord said to Satan, "Have you considered My servant Job? For there is no one like him on the earth, a blameless and upright man, fearing God and turning away from evil." Then Satan answered the Lord, "Does Job fear God for nothing? Have You not made a fence around him and his house and all that he has, on every side? You have blessed the work of his hands, and his possessions have increased in the land. But reach out with Your hand now and touch all that he has; he will certainly curse You to Your face." Then the Lord said to Satan, "Behold, all that he has is in your power; only do not reach out and put your hand on him." So Satan departed from the presence of the Lord. (Job 1:7–12 NASB)

I think this is fascinating, and it's a passage that has started to shape our view of God's goodness, even though there is still mystery and a lot we do not understand. It is evident in this passage that God would not cause any calamity whatsoever upon Job and his family, but what is interesting is that He does allow Satan to wreak havoc on Job's life. God could have told Satan, "No," but He didn't. This may hit home for you like it does for me. I know my God could have stopped the tragedies of our children, but for reasons I don't wholly understand, He did not. Here is the kicker: Our adversary believes that he is going to get Job to curse God because he gets to take so much of his life away. He thinks that people like Job (or maybe like you and me) are only in this relationship with God for what we can get out of it. He thinks that if he can take away all that Job has, Job will renounce his God. Let's see what happens:

✳ Now on the day when his sons and his daughters were eating and drinking wine in their oldest brother's house, a messenger came to Job and said, "The oxen were plowing and the female donkeys feeding beside them, and the Sabeans attacked and took them. They also killed the servants with the edge of the sword, and I alone have escaped to tell you." While he was still speaking, another came and said, "The fire of God fell from heaven and burned up the sheep and the servants and consumed them, and I alone have escaped to tell you." While he was still speaking, another also came and said, "The Chaldeans formed three units and made a raid on the camels and took them, and killed the servants with the edge of the sword, and I alone have escaped to tell you." While he was still speaking, another

60

also came and said, "Your sons and your daughters were eating and drinking wine in their oldest brother's house, and behold, a great wind came from across the wilderness and struck the four corners of the house, and it fell on the young people and they died, and I alone have escaped to tell you." Then Job got up, tore his robe, and shaved his head; then he fell to the ground and worshiped. He said,

"Naked I came from my mother's womb,

And naked I shall return there.

The Lord gave and the Lord has taken away.

Blessed be the name of the Lord."

Despite all this, Job did not sin, nor did he blame God. (Job 1:13–22 NASB)

Can you imagine this scene? Job wakes up one day, and his life is utterly destroyed in an instant! One body blow after another is delivered to Job. He loses his wealth and power. Then, the knockout punch that hits way too close to my heart: He's informed that his children are dead. Unfortunately, I can imagine the flood of emotion he must've felt. I'm sure he was in utter shock. He probably felt betrayed and confused. All the plans and dreams he had were shattered. He had to plan ten funerals and burials in an instant. I'm sure he was tempted to do exactly as Satan expected him to do. I'm sure he questioned and wondered why.

The sacrifice of praise offered at this moment is stunning and humbling for someone like me to read about. Get this: In verse 20, Job arose and tore his robe, shaved his head, fell to the ground, and worshiped! He heard the first two messages calmly, but his children were different! The implication here was not necessarily a getting up from sitting or lying. It was with inward *excitement*![12] This news lit a fire and passion under him. It's

---

[12] Robert Jamieson, A. R. Fausset, and David Brown, *Commentary Critical and Explanatory on the Whole Bible*, vol. 1 (Oak Harbor, WA: Logos Research Systems, Inc., 1997), 311.

that inward groaning and passion that rises in moments like this. It's when your soul aches and your heart throbs. Adrenaline and cortisol spike, and everything within you is moved to action. Many people (myself included, at times) will react in a fit of anger. I've punched sheetrock and punted possessions into the abyss. I've bruised knuckles pounding my fist into concrete, and I've dirtied my face falling down on the muddy ground by Kanaan's grave after a rain. These moments wreck you in the innermost parts that are impossible to reach without such deep anguish!

Job, though, immediately reacts with worship! This praise must've been the sweetest aroma in the heavenly realms. Job doesn't blame God, but he blesses the name of Jehovah (YHWH). It is astounding. When we think about the title of this book, this is precisely what it looks like to surrender to the process. Spoiler alert: The "suddenly"—or the breakthrough in his life—comes for Job, but it does not come right away. This moment was a defining moment in his life. No matter what the outside circumstances looked like, no matter what his inward emotions were doing, he offered something that cost him—praise. "Sometimes the only way through it is a hallelujah."[13]

So many people, especially type A personalities like myself, try so hard to understand everything. We will go to great lengths of Bible study, prayer, commentaries, books, sermons, mentors, and the like to understand why things happen. We become a bit like Job's friends—if you read on in the story. The pain must be because of x, y, or z. There must be a reason that caused the miscarriages and the stillbirth. I've learned through these seasons that God often wants our trust and our hearts. He's big enough to take the laments, but ultimately, He wants our praises even if we don't have the answers. I'm not suggesting that we abandon spiritual discipline—quite the contrary. You must realize that pain can lead to frustration, which God uses as an invitation to climb into His lap and sort it out with Him! It's an invitation to intimacy with our Creator!

---

[13] Benjamin William Hastings, "That's the Thing About Praise," *Benjamin William Hastings*, Capital CMG, 2022.

We embrace God and His goodness in the pain and in the frustration, and out of that, He takes our ashes and makes beauty! He does not cause these situations! He is only always good. However, just like in Job's story, He will use our heartache to sanctify us and redeem everything that was lost! If we surrender to the process in worship, we can look forward to God's goodness and the restoration of all things! We see this in the end of Job's story:

> ✳ The Lord also restored the fortunes of Job when he prayed for his friends, and the Lord increased double all that Job had. Then all his brothers, all his sisters, and all who had known him before came to him, and they ate bread with him in his house; and they sympathized with him and comforted him for all the adversities that the Lord had brought on him. And each one gave him a piece of money, and each a ring of gold. The Lord blessed the latter days of Job more than his beginning; and he had fourteen thousand sheep, six thousand camels, a thousand yoke of oxen, and a thousand female donkeys. He also had seven sons and three daughters. He named the first Jemimah, the second Keziah, and the third Keren-happuch. In all the land no women were found as beautiful as Job's daughters; and their father gave them inheritances among their brothers. After this, Job lived 140 years, and saw his sons and his grandsons, four generations. And Job died, an old man and full of days. (Job 42:10–17 NASB)

You, too, can find God's goodness in the middle of your mess.

Reflection:

~   Where have you seen or experienced God's goodness in your life?

Prayer:

Lord, thank You for Your goodness that is nourishment for my soul. Continue to show me how You never change, even though my circumstances will. Help me to hold onto Your truth spoken over me. Reveal Your goodness in a tangible way. In Jesus's name, I pray. Amen.

Chapter 6
DID GOD REALLY SAY
(NAVIGATING DISAPPOINTMENT)

He said to them, "Why are you troubled, and
why do doubts rise in your minds?"

— *Luke 24:38*

You now know God's goodness, but you might still doubt amid your pain. Did we hear God right? Did He really say we would have a child? Did you hear God right? Did He really say (fill in the blank)? Maybe you are still struggling with the questions despite knowing God is good. The Israelites struggled with this too! As they were preparing to enter the promised land (Canaan), they experienced plenty of doubts. Let's take a deep dive into this story.

Facing the Giants (Melody)

The Canaanites were one of the most powerful tribes living in the promised land. The Israelites had to cross the Jordan River to enter the promised land, where there were still giants and obstacles. They had to take that first big step of faith into the river. God miraculously parted the Jordan River waters as He had done with the Red Sea. The Israelites crossed over on dry land, and it was a reminder that God was working on their behalf. They were instructed to set up memorial stones as well. This would show future generations that God was with them and was the God of miracles.

God gave them a promise before they stepped into the waters: "This is how you will know that the living God is among you and that he will certainly drive out before the Canaanites, Hittites, Hivites, Perizzites, Girgashites, Amorites, and Jebusites. See, the ark of the covenant of the Lord of all the earth will go in to the Jordan ahead of you" (Josh. 3:10–11). The men who represented each of the tribes of Israel were holding the ark of the testimony as they stood in the Jordan while all the people crossed on dry ground. The testimony was a sign to them and others that God was with them.

Our testimony about God produces more miracles. God uses His past miracles to encourage faith in people to be expectant for more! This miracle at the Jordan River discouraged the enemy tribes living in the land. Before entering the promised land, the Israelites had the miracle of daily manna from God. Once they got to the promised land, the manna stopped. They began to enjoy the fruit of the land of Canaan. God had told Joshua He would be with him and defeat the enemies. God had given him a promise that Joshua could rest his faith on. Faith sees what is still unseen! The Lord came through for Joshua, and the people defeated city by city.

Before the Israelites crossed over into the promised land, they sent spies to scope it out. At the time, Joshua and Caleb were the only ones who brought back positive reports. The other spies discouraged the people and only focused on all the giants in the land. The Lord had already declared that He was giving them the land, but they chose to focus on the wrong thing!

✱ Moses gave the men these instructions as he sent them out to explore the land: "Go north through the Negev into the hill country. See what the land is like, and find out whether the people living there are strong or weak, few or many. See what kind of land they live in. Is it good or bad? Do their towns have walls, or are they unprotected like open camps? Is the soil fertile or poor? Are there many trees? Do your best to bring back samples of the crops you see." (It happened to be the season for harvesting the first ripe grapes.)

(Num. 13:17–20 NLT)

Initially, the Israelites knew that God had said the promised land was theirs, but they gave in to the adverse reports, forgetting and not believing what God had said. They were disappointed when they heard of the giants.

✶ After exploring the land for forty days, the men returned to Moses, Aaron, and the whole community of Israel at Kadesh in the wilderness of Paran. They reported to the whole community what they had seen and showed them the fruit they had taken from the land. This was their report to Moses: "We entered the land you sent us to explore, and it is indeed a bountiful country—a land flowing with milk and honey. Here is the kind of fruit it produces. But the people living there are powerful, and their towns are large and fortified. We even saw giants there, the descendants of Anak! The Amalekites live in the Negev, and the Hittites, Jebusites, and Amorites live in the hill country. The Canaanites live along the coast of the Mediterranean Sea and along the Jordan Valley." But Caleb tried to quiet the people as they stood before Moses. "Let's go at once to take the land," he said. "We can certainly conquer it!" But the other men who had explored the land with him disagreed. "We can't go up against them! They are stronger than we are!" So they spread this bad report about the land among the Israelites: "The land we traveled through and explored will devour anyone who goes to live there. All the people we saw were huge. We even saw giants there, the descendants of Anak. Next to them we felt like grasshoppers, and that's what they thought, too!" (Num. 13:25–33 NLT)

They focused on their problems, the giants. They forgot what God said and chose to live in fear. Because of that, that generation did not get to enter the promised land, but Joshua and Caleb did!

✳ Two of the men who had explored the land, Joshua son of Nun and Caleb son of Jephunneh, tore their clothing. They said to all the people of Israel, "The land we traveled through and explored is a wonderful land! And if the Lord is pleased with us, he will bring us safely into that land and give it to us. It is a rich land flowing with milk and honey. Do not rebel against the Lord, and don't be afraid of the people of the land. They are only helpless prey to us! They have no protection, but the Lord is with us! Don't be afraid of them!"

But the whole community began to talk about stoning Joshua and Caleb. Then the glorious presence of the Lord appeared to all the Israelites at the Tabernacle. And the Lord said to Moses, "How long will these people treat me with contempt? Will they never believe me, even after all the miraculous signs I have done among them? I will disown them and destroy them with a plague. Then I will make you into a nation greater and mightier than they are!" (Num. 14:6–12 NLT)

Just because God was with Joshua and Caleb doesn't mean there were no battles, obstacles, pain, or disappointment. There were many. They probably saw many family members die and not enter the promised land with them. They had to trust and surrender their agendas to God. They had to ask God for help, believe what He said was true, and obey it.

Dealing with Doubt (Melody) ✳ ━━━━━━━━━━━━━

There were still many times in the next two years after Kanaan's passing when I struggled to figure out what I was supposed to do since I still did not have children here to nourish and raise. I was so disappointed. I had always wanted to be a stay-at-home mom, have a homestead, and do business from home. The hopes for that were changing, and I was struggling to even enjoy life. Even small daily tasks seemed too much for me, such as:

- making homemade meals like I used to (I didn't have a desire or appetite to)
- getting up early and ready for the day
- cleaning the house well
- being motivated by passions I once had

Pain and disappointment had changed me. It had shaped me differently.

I didn't have any excitement for life even though I had Jesus by my side every single day. It was as though I had to start my life over again. Many days, I struggled to open my Bible, listen to worship music, etc. I always felt fatigued. I tried to fill my time with things that seemed important to me, but they were not right for that season.

As the months passed, most people stopped reaching out. I felt I had to remind the world I had a precious son in Heaven, and he was to be acknowledged. No one else would carry his legacy here except us. It was a hard truth, but it helped us understand that no one else would do that because he wasn't anyone else's son. Only four family members got to see and meet him, which was one of my biggest regrets. It was painful.

I began to learn more about disappointment. I had been disappointed not just once but three times in our quest to have biological children. It was hard to wrap my mind around it. This disappointment was something the enemy used to put us in a dark victim hole (totally justifiable at the time), but not where we were supposed to go with our disappointment. We were supposed to go to God. I tried, and it was hard. I would surrender it, thinking I had entirely given it to God, and then realize later that I had not wholly. We will talk about our journey of surrender in a later chapter.

A friend from ministry school told me that God (as an artist) uses all the colors of our lives to create something beautiful. When things seem to be going well (colorful and bright), some gray and black enter (loss, grief, disappointments, crisis) our life (color palate). Naturally, we are nervous about God using those colors, thinking it will destroy the piece of art. But it is the opposite. His bright colors (light) overpower the dark ones, yet you can still see some of the grays and blacks as reminders of what He has brought you through to make a work of art: you. It has taken me a while to be okay with that.

As we write this book, I am thirty years old, and it's hard sometimes not to look back and be sad about some things that should have been but are not how we had hoped. I also choose to look at this time in my life and feel grateful for all the memories, God encounters, faithfulness, blessings, and hope for our future. I should have all our kiddos here on this side of Heaven and not just our daughter (adopted). Life, however, is not predictable, and we can't control it. No matter how much we plan, we do not get to know how things will turn out.

There will always be an opportunity for disappointment in our lives, sometimes justifiable, like Job and many others in the Bible. What did many of those people do? They surrendered and trusted God. Trusting God was a concept I thought wasn't something you did. I thought it was more something you just said. But trusting God meant not having DOUBT in what God wanted to do in my life and my circumstances. I realized I had unbelief in God's promises, and it took me a long time to recognize that doubting God was sinful. It allowed me to be swayed too much by our circumstances. "But when you ask, you must believe and not doubt, because the one who doubts is like a wave of the sea, blown and tossed by the wind" (James 1:6). Once I realized the wind of my circumstances was tossing me, I could repent, be forgiven for doubting, and continue to believe what God had said.

This verse was a huge perspective shift for me: "Let us strip off every weight that slows us down, especially the sin that so easily trips us up. And let us run with endurance the race God has set before us" (Heb. 12:1 NLT). One commentary says:

✷ The sin which doth so easily beset us—Greek, "sin which easily stands around us"; so Luther, "which always so clings to us": "sinful propensity always surrounding us, ever present and ready" [Wahl]. It is not primarily "the sin," &c., but sin in general, with, however, special reference to "apostasy," against which he had already warned them, as one to which they might gradually be seduced; the besetting sin of the Hebrews, unbelief.[14]

I realized that doubt and unbelief of God's promises were sin. Doubt entangles you and distracts you. As the commentary above states, this is a sin that is always present and ready, waiting for us. As speaking to one specific sin, it would speak to the context of the sin of unbelief and doubt of God's promises. This was a light bulb moment for me because I had let disappointment teach me in a way that caused me to doubt what God had said.

God has given us several personal words in our lives. The Holy Spirit often brought up the same word because He knew there would be a battle around it. We need to be constantly reminded that God stays true to His promises and is faithful. There would be many pruning and character

[14]

Chapter Six

Robert Jamieson, A. R. Fausset, and David Brown, *Commentary Critical and Explanatory on the Whole Bible*, vol. 2 (Oak Harbor, WA: Logos Research Systems, Inc., 1997), 475.

Chapter Seven

·

alterations in our journey. It was like being recreated and saying goodbye to thinking the old way. The "what about me" and "why me" ways of thought had been a comfort in my victim mindset and made everything I was going through and feeling justifiable. However, Jesus suffered greatly, and He would have been justified if He had acted a certain way, but He didn't give in to those temptations from the enemy. He didn't compare, He didn't have a victim mentality, and He didn't try to skip past pain. He endured for all of us. He persevered because He knew His Father's promises. Just like Jesus—and just like Joshua and Caleb—we had to learn to believe God's promises and not have doubt that He would stay faithful to His word to us.

A Spirit of Foreboding (David)

I know there can be a lot of skepticism and opinions around "prophetic words" and God's promises for today. Let me boil it down in this simple way. Prophetic words are meant to encourage and foretell the future. They shouldn't go against God's Word or tear others down. I have looked back and realized how encouraging all the words I have received have been. It's remarkable how God has used people we know and do not know to encourage us. Seeing some things come to pass has been even more encouraging. We have experienced and seen words and dreams come to pass. Some of those things have taken years, and others are still yet to come. I have learned to be ready at any time for what God has said will happen. It's living in the now, but not yet! Why not? Today could be the day!

Contending with hope is hard. I remember years back when we had received words from God saying we would have children and full-term babies and wounds from the past would be healed. When we got pregnant with Kanaan, we thought it was part of the fulfillment of that word. We were so sure of it. However, his story ended up being different. We ended up with more trauma from his passing. Our current circumstances at that time made us question God's word for us and His goodness. However, God never changes. We had to take time to process that and honestly believe that what He said would come to pass.

We must navigate disappointment with God and turn face-to-face with Him. It's not about performing perfectly so that God can break through. That doesn't work! Disappointment can get you to try to perform, hoping for a different outcome. The Israelites did a lot of this. God made promises to them, but when they encountered opposition, they forgot what God had said.

Foreboding means an impending sense of doom. This spirit makes you feel like something is always about to go wrong. Even on a good day, you feel like a bad day is coming. The Israelites had things go wrong before, and some almost expected bad things to happen before they did! What if we did that in a positive way?

The Apostle Paul discusses this spirit: "We use God's mighty weapons, not worldly weapons, to knock down the strongholds of human reasoning and to destroy false arguments" (2 Cor. 10:4 NLT).

We need to destroy these false arguments and speculations. Speculations are the "what ifs" caused by this spirit of foreboding. What if you don't make it to your promised land? What if your children get kidnapped, raped, or molested? What if you can't pay your rent? What if the doctor says you have cancer?

When this spirit works in you, the "what ifs" are NEVER positive. You never think, what if my wife is pregnant with twins? What if the reason my boss called me in was to give me a raise? Those are optimistic, hope-filled what-ifs.

We have mighty weapons against this spirit of foreboding. But first, we must reject this spirit by understanding the source of these thoughts. This spirit is an intrusion, and these are not our own thoughts. Tell that spirit to go to hell!

The truth is something is about to go right. "And we know that in all things God works for the good of those who love him, who have been called according to his purpose" (Rom. 8:28). Believe it and create a highway of blessing.

Wrestle with the friction of disappointment. It costs something to pray again and to believe again. In these moments, this is another opportunity to give God something that costs you, and it's a flat-out heavyweight fight! If we allow disappointment to become chronic, we will always judge God and His promises by what He did not do. If the only thoughts we ever entertain are about what hasn't happened, we empower unbelief and create a measure and a lifestyle of disappointment and failure. Disappointment is a disease that can infect us and attract a foreboding spirit. We can't be trusted with the fulfillment of life if we can't learn to navigate disappointment. Navigating disappointment gives us access to more significant breakthroughs.

You can apply these truths to any part of your walk and your life. Don't think for a second that disappointment and foreboding can't creep into any part of your life if you're not on guard and warring against it with the Holy Spirit and with God's Word! Maybe you can identify with parts of our story about dealing with extreme disappointment, and maybe you can't. It's okay either way and quite frankly, we hope you can't—because it was horrific on many levels.

Wrestling with Disappointment (David) ✳━━━━━━━━━

In America, almost everyone can identify with a good old-fashioned underdog story. On the surface, it is fun and refreshing, but if you look a bit deeper, almost all these stories that we love start with one person overcoming disappointment and foreboding. When your team loses, and you get heartbroken so many times, it's easy to develop a negative attitude toward the team, the athletes, the coaches, and even the city or the state! Even when things are going well, people find it hard to enjoy life because (in their words) they are "waiting for the other shoe to drop." That is a classic manifestation of the foreboding spirit that is at work in something seemingly not of utmost importance. Be careful, though, friends. I've seen it start there, and if it goes unchecked, it affects families, communities, and whole cities! I would know; I'm a Vikings fan. I will save you from reading another story about the Vikings at this time, though. You see, when disappointment sets into any area of your life, it demands to be wrestled with. It's not going to go away without a fight! It doesn't matter if it's delay at work, infertility, marital issues, family struggles, or even your favorite sports team; the battle is there, and you must decide to engage with it!

I love the sport of wrestling. It's probably the oldest sport of all time and one of the few sports mentioned in the Bible. It's legal hand-to-hand combat. The thrill of victory and the agony of defeat is yours alone. There are no teammates to blame or funny bounces of an odd-shaped ball. You get out of the sport exactly what you put into it, and there is little left to chance. It's the most brutal, most challenging sport you could engage in, but also the most rewarding. God has used the sport of wrestling in my life to help shape me into the man I am today, and He has also used it to hone my leadership skills.

In my mid-twenties, I got an incredible opportunity to be the head coach of our local high school wrestling program. It is the school I graduated from, so it was a tremendous opportunity to give back to the community that gave me so much. I quickly realized that disappointment had attached itself to this group of young men and that a foreboding spirit was not only welcome in that wrestling room but was honored and celebrated. I heard story after story of how each guy and the team almost made it but fell short. There was every excuse in the book; some were very valid!

"I would've, but I had a terrible injury! I would've, but the referee made a bad call! I would've, but my coach failed me!" they exclaimed frequently. The worst one I heard, though (and this was an infection in the whole city), was, "If things are going great, just wait, it will get messed up somehow. That's just what happens to us here." It broke my heart, but they believed it. Their parents and family thought it; quite frankly, the conference, section, and state believed it too!

God showed me this immediately, and I'm so grateful because I knew what I had to attack. The moment the athletic director reached out his hand and gave me the keys to the wrestling room, the Lord whispered, "As you take the keys, take authority!" I was struck at that moment because I realized that I now had a level of dominion and authority to shape these young men and instill in them a confidence that God could do great things in and through them.

I also realized that I needed reinforcements. I called specific friends and family and asked if they'd come alongside me to help invest in these guys, and they were all excited! God helped me put together one of Minnesota's most amazing coaching staffs, and it wasn't because I was on it! I had elite wrestling talent and top-notch motivation and strategy guys. It felt a bit like the Avengers! We set out for our first season and had some success, but we also had our share of bumps and bruises along the way. We battled significant injuries and some heartbreaking losses, but through that, we started to chip away at the foreboding spirit.

Through the first couple of years, we worked hard to hone technique, be in great shape, and put the team in the best position to win matches and develop. I don't want to downplay any of that because it was all essential in our journey, but we recognized God's hand in all of this, and we felt led to pray! In a public school setting, we would pray before every event as a team. It was optional, of course, but I don't remember a single guy missing it. It became a part of the pre-match routine that they looked forward to! We would invite God in, give Him glory, and ask Him for wisdom and favor. We prayed for safety from injuries and favor with the matchups and the calls. We prayed for peace and, most of all, that our wrestling would be considered worship in the heavens. I believe God used that to begin to break strongholds in our guys, their families, and the community. Through those moments, things shifted. They started to believe that God was for them and that good things could happen. They began to celebrate each other and believe in the direction we were heading.

In the 2020-2021 season, we faced some of the most difficult challenges yet. It felt like we were getting so close to a breakthrough that the enemy did his best to discourage the whole group. We dealt with injuries, losses, and the threat of COVID-19 shutdowns stealing the entire season. We picked our theme as we did every year, but in the face of adversity and uncertainty, this one was simple yet so prophetic and profound. It was one word: Believe! When anyone felt that familiar foreboding spirit telling them, "Here we go again," we reminded and encouraged one another: Believe!

I don't mean to paint any picture that prayer fixes everything or that God is some genie granting wishes. He's not, and the road certainly wasn't easy! In this case, God was doing something more significant than wrestling, but wrestling was the language our guys could understand. That is another attribute of God that is astounding! He comes to our level and speaks our language. He was molding and shaping men to believe in Him. He was using wrestling as a simulation for life off the mat. Many of those guys are now or are soon-to-be husbands, dads, and leaders! This season of their lives taught all of us that bad things happen, and things can look murky. We can take hard losses and have things go wrong but still pick ourselves up, give God our ashes, and let Him make something beautiful out of them.

Now, picture the scene. This high school had never won a state championship in any sport, and, at the time of writing this, they haven't again. No one (including many of us at the beginning of the season) thought this team could do it! But as we continued to control what we could control and give the rest to God, we saw giant after giant fall. We beat a rival we hadn't beaten since I was an athlete to win the section. We had extreme favor with the matchups on the road to the championship. When we reached the state tournament, we saw the number one-ranked team go down in the semi-finals as we advanced on the other side of the bracket.

There we were—in the state championship match! Standing before us was a team that had just slain Goliath, and they were oozing with confidence. Quite frankly, so were we. We had seen too much go our way.

The disappointment was broken off, and the foreboding spirit was gone. We were free! Sitting in that corner was a surreal moment, watching this come to fruition. We lost the first three matches in a row! In the past, I'd have to get up and stir the guys up and remind them to believe, but not this time. They were battle-tested, and they trusted in the next guy. They believed, even down three matches to zero. The momentum started to shift in front of my eyes. We did not lose another match until we already had the dual locked up. It didn't look like the state championship match. It looked like we were way better that day! It wasn't even close. It was a blowout, and we were state champions! So many emotions flooded over everyone in the following moments, days, and even weeks. We went from something special to something historic. We went from just a good season to state championship signage at all corners of our little town! It was forever. It was a breakthrough. It was God.

God still does the improbable. He still does the impossible. Will you wrestle with the friction of disappointment long enough to win?

Stay In the Fight (David) ✳━━━━━━━━━━━━━━━━

That state championship moment was and still is a testimony to me as we journey along our way. Believe it or not, Kanaan got to "watch" that from his mommy's belly. It wasn't too long after that he went home to Jesus. As I was reflecting on the roller coaster of life, God gave me an excellent picture I'd like to share with you to close this chapter. It's easy to forget moments like the state championship when I'm in the despair of losing my son. ***It's easy to forget the testimony when we are in the middle of a test.*** We must wrestle with the friction of disappointment. We must break off and break agreement with foreboding and familiar spirits. We have to stay in the fight.

The Lord showed me a vision of myself walking toward a cage to engage in a UFC-type fight or battle. I crawled into the cage, and He locked the door behind me. It felt scary and intimidating at the moment, but His peace came when He spoke: "The fight is against disappointment. You will emerge the victor if you don't leave the cage." In other words, if you refuse to let disappointment make you get out of the fight, you win. Disappointment might hit you or even knock you down, but keep going to battle, armed with God's promises. It's the only way to outlast and leave the wrestling match of disappointment with your hand raised!

Reflection:
~ Is there any place in your life where you feel you are partnering with disappointment or a foreboding spirit?

Prayer:
Father God, I recognize and ask for Your forgiveness in partnering with disappointment and foreboding. I ask that You change the way I think and help me be filled with the thoughts of Christ. Help me to process the disappointment I have experienced and move toward hope. In Jesus's name, I pray. Amen.

Chapter 7
OVERCOMING TRAUMA
(FINDING FREEDOM)

The Lord is close to the brokenhearted and
saves those who are crushed in spirit.

— *Psalm 34:18*

Trauma. If you have a gut reaction to that word, maybe you've experienced it. The word is often used but, sadly, little understood. After facing severe loss, some people go years acting in odd ways or having seemingly out-of-character reactions. Trauma affects us to our core.

Under the Surface (David)

There I was, trembling on the floor in a puddle of sweat and tears. When I came to my senses, I had no idea how I got there. Melody was crying and comforting me, but I had nothing left. The wound caused by all the trauma just felt too big to heal. This moment took place months after Kanaan went to be with Jesus, and at times, it felt like I was no further down the journey of grief. "Maybe I am getting worse," I thought. "What if I actually can't make it through this? What is going on, and how did I get here?"

Let me back up just a little bit that day. It probably started with something simple, like a coworker telling me something insensitive like, "You just wait until you have kids; I only got (blank) hours of sleep last night!" I brushed it off. It hurts, but I'm professional, and I just quietly removed myself from the situation and retreated to my office to stare at a photo of my dead son. "I do have kids," I thought to myself. "They are my deposits in Heaven. And I beg to differ; I have just as much trouble sleeping as you do."

Rant over, back to work. Later that same afternoon, somebody brought their kids into the office. I don't have any problem with that or anything against those people! But in my current state, it was hard to watch everyone so extravagantly love other people's kids. Again, it was rarely out of jealousy or resentment. It was just out of a place of deep hurt that others didn't understand. It should be my kids, too, but life isn't fair. I thought to myself, "My kids are getting to play with their heavenly Father," and it brought a moment of reprieve and allowed me to get back to work.

The work day dragged on, and the end of the day came. I slammed my laptop shut and tossed it in my backpack. I made the short trek home to find my beautiful wife crying on the couch. She's had moments like I had today, too, but in different forms. Immediately, I go into comfort mode. We pray, talk, cry, and give it to God again. I couldn't talk about my day because it would upset her. I felt like I had nowhere to go. Nobody got it. Everybody was trying to fix me and heal me, but the wound was open and oozing. The bandages weren't cutting it. I needed more profound healing, but unfortunately, I couldn't find it in friends and family who didn't understand. Everything was bubbling under the surface because I had nowhere to go with it. I needed surgery and antibiotics, but it seemed my circle was only equipped to offer salt in the open wound. Sure, that might be good for it, but it was so painful that I couldn't receive it.

Later that night, before bed, we were talking with some loved ones on the phone, and I remember somebody saying they had a dream about our children in Heaven. That sounded like an excellent idea, and it's one I had thought of often. The statement wasn't wrong or insensitive. But that's how the nuances and complexities of grief and trauma work. Although the words were accurate, and I agreed with the statement, I could no longer take the niceties and the bandages people were offering. It wasn't fair; they didn't understand, and I wanted to quit talking about it for a while. That was the trigger at that moment. On top of everything else that day, that's all it took. Flashbacks flooded my mind. It was like I was there again. I was back in a cold white hospital room where we were told that Kanaan was small and that his condition was incompatible with life. I was back in the hospital room where I learned of the loss of my first daughter and the Viking's loss at the same moment. I was back in the birth center where the only cries were from us because our dead son couldn't cry. I was back with a shovel in hand, putting my son's ashes in the ground. I was even back to losses of good friends I had in high school. I was back to the day we felt we had to give up our dream of having a hobby farm and goats. I was back to the day we had to rehome our beautiful puppy, who we had raised from four weeks old on goat milk. I was back to losses of wrestling matches and football games I went through as a youth. All in one moment, when that trigger was pulled, it was all back—overwhelmingly back and sharper than ever.

I threw my fist through the bedroom sheetrock and proceeded to convulse and tremble on the floor with these memories rolling like a virtual reality movie, but it wasn't virtual. It scared my wife, but I was scared too. I didn't feel like I could be the comforter anymore because I needed comfort as much as I needed my next breath. It was an out-of-body experience because all I remember after that was Melody crouching over me, crying and praying. I finally came to my senses and calmed down. We hugged, embraced, and went back to bed, but we couldn't sleep. I'm told that's what it's like when you "have kids."

The original Greek word from which we get our English word trauma is literally translated as "wound." Trauma does precisely what I described above. It wounds you to the point that any aid feels painful and stings. Trauma to your body, brain, or both requires special treatment for the mind, body, and spirit!

Taking Thoughts Captive (Melody) ✴━━━━━━━━━━━━

What we were dealing with was trauma and Post-Traumatic Stress Disorder (PTSD)—a typical reaction to traumatic events—as well as postpartum depression for me. Flashbacks, panic attacks, emotional numbness, anxiety, depression, irritability, insomnia, not being able to focus, isolation, and unhealthy habits stemmed from the trauma. I remember so many times that triggers would bring flashbacks and deep heartache. After having Kanaan, I went through all the things a new mom experiences: producing milk, having to heal physically from birth, sleepless nights, etc. There was a lot of emotional numbness during this time for me. I lost interest in just about all the things I was doing before in life. My passions disappeared, my interest in health and wellness decreased as I lost my appetite, and I let my body suffer. Lots of relationships changed. When you feel numb after the death of a child, someone you deeply loved, all the joy can feel sucked out of you. It's sometimes hard to be happy, excited, or even sad. Numbness overtakes you, and you have no emotion in the moment.

I went through a short season of that and then an extended season of anxiety and depression. I fell into a crippling freeze or flight mode. As David mentioned, I remembered the other losses we experienced, like when we rehomed our beautiful dog, Liberty, due to changes at work and family dynamics. After she was gone, David felt like he had lost another thing in his life, which hurt. He said, "I can't lose anything else right now." It hadn't dawned on me until then that each thing that was taken away or lost in this season made it feel like we were losing Kanaan all over again. This feeling didn't last forever, but in the fresh days of grief, it felt like it would.

According to Psychology Today, "Trauma can affect your brain's emotion networks to make you overreact or under-react to stressful situations. Trauma creates fixed neural networks that are isolated from other parts of your brain and resistant to change."[15]

Baby showers and pregnancy announcements were triggers for me. What I had experienced had tainted how I thought future events would go. I had anxiety about going to baby showers because I didn't want to break down in front of everyone or relive the pain and loss I had experienced. I remember opening a baby shower invite from someone I knew and immediately feeling a jolt in my chest and a tightening in my jaw to keep from crying. I was happy for that person but sad for my situation. I had to give myself grace in those times when I knew I could not make it through. It would be like reliving the baby shower I had for Kanaan, only to lose him the week after. As time went on, I knew that using that same excuse would not help me overcome the pain I had experienced.

There is a time and a season to guard your heart as you are in the process of grief and healing. You don't have to push yourself to the limits, but you still want people to know you love and care about them even if you can't show up physically. I had to say goodbye to some social media and block specific profiles and pages for a time because I couldn't constantly be bombarded with pregnancy announcements. It wasn't helpful at that time in my journey. At the same time, I didn't want to be the last one to know if someone close to me was pregnant because that was hurtful to find out last. It was simply the reality of what I was living with. It would sting, but at some point, I would have to move on from it to be free. There was emotional, spiritual, and physical trauma I had to work through and heal from. Each piece has been such a journey. I had to get to such a low spot in my life that I knew only God could get me out of the pit, just like Joseph (see Genesis 37). I had to choose not to let emotions control me. They were supposed to

---

[15] "Understanding the Trauma Brain," Psychology Today, accessed February 6, 2025, https://www.psychologytoday.com/us/blog/the-mindful-self-express/202106/understanding-the-trauma-brain.

be like a check engine light that comes on—a clue to realize something must be addressed or processed.

I didn't only experience emotional repercussions. Physically, I got sick, lost too much weight, my thyroid and hormones got out of whack, I had severe fatigue, and I got physically weak. Trauma affects every part of us. But did you know the effects of trauma don't have to be permanent?

* After any type of trauma (from combat to car accidents, natural disasters to domestic violence, sexual assault to child abuse), the brain and body change. Every cell records memories and every embedded, trauma-related neuropathway has the opportunity to repeatedly reactivate. Sometimes the alterations these imprints create are transitory, the small glitch of disruptive dreams and moods that subside in a few weeks. In other situations the changes evolve into readily apparent symptoms that impair function and present in ways that interfere with jobs, friendships, and relationships. . . . While changes to the brain can seem, on the surface, disastrous and representative of permanent damage, the truth is that all of these alterations can be reversed. The amygdala can learn to relax; the hippocampus can resume proper memory consolidation; the nervous system can recommence its easy flow between reactive and restorative modes. The key to achieving a state of neutrality and then healing lies in reprograming the body and mind.[16]

As a believer, how do you heal from trauma when you have gone through something life-changing? "We demolish arguments and every pretension that sets itself up against the knowledge of God, and we take captive every thought to make it obedient to Christ" (2 Cor. 10:5). We take our thoughts captive and give our experiences to God. Because trauma

---

[16] "How Trauma Changes the Brain," Boston Clinical Trials, accessed February 6, 2025, https://www.bostontrials.com/how-trauma-changes-the-brain/.

increases fear and anxiety, it was even more crucial to learn to rewire how I was thinking. Over time, I finally got to the point where the memories and images no longer contained so much pain and sadness. Time spent in prayer and worship, Scripture, encouraging words from people God brought into our lives, and learning God's character helped us through this time. Every day was different, and we had to make a daily choice to heal.

Releasing Strongholds (Melody) ✳━━━━━━━━━━━━

Spiritually, I felt wounded. God's promises and words on our lives seemed so far away and like an impossible story. Some sleepless nights were filled with crying until I had exhausted myself. Isolation affected my relationships in many ways because it felt like no one could understand. Some isolation was necessary for me in the beginning, but it got to a point where what had previously guarded me from constant hurt was preventing me from now accepting love. It was hard to let others in who had said or done offensive or hurtful things, even if they had no idea. People who were insensitive or even playing the victim themselves did not help because they had never even had a conversation with me to try and understand why I was reacting the way I was. They say sometimes the worst wounds are the ones you cannot see. Isolating became my coping method. Fear and worry intertwined with it. I tried to shelter my broken heart because I didn't want more wounding. Triggers led me to isolate and only trust who I felt could understand me and my situation.

On the flip side, some people reached out who genuinely cared, and I felt I could be vulnerable and honest with them. I remember going to a mom's event one day. Multiple people (out of the kindness of their hearts) invited me, but as I left that day, I cried all the way home. It simply was not something I was ready for, and it didn't apply to me yet. The lesson was about disciplining kids and raising kids in a God-honoring manner. That wasn't me yet. It was hard to accept that.

People started not to reach out as much, and I slowly fell into anxiety and depression. It was one of the lowest times of my life, besides when I lost a best friend to suicide in high school. Sometimes, you have to go through a season of something dark in order to recognize and see the light. I recognized that I had experienced trauma, and I needed freedom and healing from it. I didn't want to allow it to control my life anymore. I wanted to put in the work and experience healing. I wanted to break its stronghold on my life and future.

✶   In his book *Supernatural Freedom from the Captivity of Trauma*, Mike Hutchings says:

> When we have a stronghold full of lies based upon traumatic experiences, it not only impacts and speaks to our present, it also speaks to our future causing us to live with a mental stronghold that says that because of our past history we can only expect bad things to happen to us in the future. With this kind of thinking, we are always waiting for the next bad thing to happen. Our imagination and speculation is not positive but negative, which affects our hope, our faith, and how we believe our future will be.[17]

I was in ministry school during this time, and I am so grateful for it to this day. It was one thing that helped pull me back into encountering God and His Word. Being in a community of believers who had been through hard things and gotten through them with God was what I needed to be around. My faith, hope, and beliefs were being tested, and I needed a community to help pray with me and hold me up—just like Aaron holding Moses's arms (see Exodus 17).

God encountered me one day as I was sitting still in His presence. I experienced a vision as I sat there. I saw a picture of someone hiking up a mountain. She had on a large, weighted backpack and all her gear. The

---

[17] Mike Hutchings, Supernatural Freedom from the Captivity of Trauma (Destiny Image Publishers, 2021), 81.

Lord stood there as she made it to the top of the mountain. She took off her backpack and everything she had been carrying. She set it at the feet of Jesus, turned around, and walked down the mountain. She left it all at the top and had a lighter load as she walked away. That was me. I was carrying all these soul injuries. My grief, losses, pain, trauma, heartache, anger, sadness, envy, and disappointment were things I was never meant to carry. I was meant to give them to God—every day, every moment. I was meant to be free. Here is the truth: We need comfort from God to heal our trauma and pain so that we can step out into unfamiliar places. God will give you a garment of praise instead of heaviness. It was time for me to let that heaviness down. It took me a couple of years to get to that point. If I was willing to lay down and ask God to heal and remove the trauma, He would get the glory!

Sometimes, amid trauma, our identity can be of a victim or an oppressed person. But that's not our true identity. Our identity is supposed to be a victor and overcomer in Christ. We then have the enemy's feet under ours instead of ours under his. Your pain becomes your purpose in healing. I had to take the step to finally talk out the trauma, continuing to give it to the Lord until I felt like I had released it. This was the beginning of cleansing every area of my life.

Healing Body, Soul, and Spirit (David)

Trauma is an actual physical and mental condition. It is getting more and more attention from doctors, surgeons, and even more holistic natural providers. According to the Mayo Clinic, "Post-traumatic stress disorder (PTSD) is a mental health condition that's caused by an extremely stressful or terrifying event."[18] Symptoms can include:

- persistent negative thoughts or emotions, such as fear, anger, guilt, or shame

---

[18] "Post-traumatic stress disorder (PTSD)," Mayo Clinic, accessed February 14, 2025, https://www.mayoclinic.org/diseases-conditions/post-traumatic-stress-disorder/symptoms-causes/syc-20355967.

- unwanted memories or nightmares of the trauma
- avoiding situations that remind the person of the trauma
- heightened reactions, anxiety, or depressed mood
- sleep problems
- feeling detached or numb
- being easily startled
- reckless or self-destructive behavior
- problems concentrating

PTSD can develop after many types of traumatic events, including:
- violent personal assaults
- natural or human-caused disasters
- accidents
- combat
- sexual assault
- child abuse
- domestic violence

I always had this false notion that PTSD and trauma-related issues only apply to veterans coming back from war. Although it applies to our military, after losing Kanaan and experiencing things like we described at the beginning of this chapter, I realized that many people deal with trauma whether it's diagnosed as PTSD or not. You cannot fight an enemy that you do not acknowledge is there. Melody and I realized that these events were traumatizing and that they left wounds that needed special care. Clichés weren't going to work. Religion wasn't going to work. Medication (although helpful and necessary at times) wasn't going to fix the root of the problem. The hard part about trauma is that it is usually multi-faceted. It can be physical, spiritual, mental, or emotional, but in my experience, real trauma touches all those things! The problem with the Western medical system and even religion is that it only addresses one part of the human. We are spirit, soul, and body in this earthly experience, and all of those must be healed first to truly recover and be whole.

The Greek word used in the New Testament for salvation is sozo. We think of salvation as forgiving sins, but sozo goes way beyond that. According to Strong's Concordance, sozo "is used to describe both physical and spiritual salvation. Physically, it can refer to healing from illness or rescue from danger."[19] Although there are treatments for PTSD and trauma, I've found the only thing that genuinely has worked is an encounter with Jesus. When Jesus healed in His ministry, He healed body, soul, and spirit. His healings were profound. They were sozo (salvation).

When we are held captive to a lie of the stronghold of trauma, there is harm to our health. If we want freedom, we must replace lies with God's truth.

God's Healing Touch (Melody) ✳━━━━━━━━━━━━━━

The woman who touched Jesus's cloak received complete healing. "Just then a woman who had been subject to bleeding for twelve years came up behind him and touched the edge of his cloak. She said to herself, 'If I only touch his cloak, I will be healed'" (Matt. 9:20–21).

This woman had not just received healing physically but also experienced deliverance and freedom. Sozo in her life connected her to Heaven's truth. Jesus changed her and healed her trauma; she walked in freedom. Imagine the traumatic experiences she probably went through. People ignored her because she was seen as unclean. She was told, "Sorry, there is nothing we can do" for her physical issue. She was neglected by her family and the people she once had in her life. Fear of what people would say and think and feeling unworthy probably played into her experience of trauma. She even knew the risk of getting close to people, especially Jesus, in front of a crowd. But she took the risk. She probably had a fear flare up

---

[19] "Sozo," Bible Hub, accessed February 6, 2025, https://biblehub.com/greek/4982.htm.

as she decided to reach for His cloak. But she pressed through, and it was the best decision of her life. She no longer experienced self-pity or a victim mentality. She no longer experienced beliefs and behaviors that enslaved her. She had experienced sozo.

While reading this story, I realized that in the same way God spoke a word to her, God had spoken a word to us. Before we had Kanaan, a person of faith we highly respect shared a word they believed God spoke to them about us. God said He would heal the trauma that was in my womb from the pregnancy losses I had experienced. Now, we were pressing in for God to heal the trauma from the stillbirth of Kanaan. Through a couple of SOZO sessions, I did find healing and freedom. (If you're unfamiliar, simply put, a SOZO session is directed prayer for deliverance and healing, guided by the Holy Spirit and leading to an encounter with Jesus.) I didn't necessarily receive healing all at once or even in one year, but God continued to heal me emotionally, spiritually, and physically. I still had hope and believed that He could and He would.

Complete Healing (David) ✴━━━━━━━━━━━━━━━

There are many examples of sozo healing in the Bible, but I want to explore a couple. In Mark 2, four friends lower a paralyzed man through the roof to get healed. Picture the scene with me for a second. Jesus was in a packed house, and there was no way you could fit another body in the building. This man is desperate for healing, but he's helpless. His friends are some amazing friends! Who wouldn't want to have friends that put you on a stretcher and carry you to Jesus no matter the obstacle—even if they have to tear off the roof? Can you imagine being in that meeting, and out of the corner of your eye, you see daylight coming through the roof? You pause for a second, and it dawns on you: Five men are on top of the roof, forcing their way to Jesus. The whole scene plays out, and they lower this paralyzed man through the roof of the home, and he's lying there.

Jesus says something here that is puzzling to the people in the room.

In Mark 2:5, Jesus sees their faith. Let's pause there for a moment. Many people skip over this as they read, but it's essential. It's important enough to the story that Mark includes the fact that even Jesus takes notice of their faith. He sees their faith! I imagine it warms His heart a bit, and maybe He smirked or chuckled at this moment but then said, "Son, your sins are forgiven." Staggering. Everyone expected physical healing, and He says your sins are forgiven.

Now, the religious people are up in arms, and they question Jesus. It's probably the same question we'd have. They ask why He is forgiving sins. "Now some teachers of the law were sitting there, thinking to themselves, 'Why does this fellow talk like that? He's blaspheming! Who can forgive sins but God alone?'" (Mark 2:6–7). Jesus senses their questions in Spirit, and He replies in verse 9, "Which is easier: to say to this paralyzed man, 'Your sins are forgiven,' or to say, 'Get up, take your mat and walk?'" He explains His authority and then tells the man, "Get up, take your mat and go home!" (Mark 2:11).

You see this throughout Jesus's ministry, but what strikes me here is this: Jesus doesn't just heal the man physically. He heals him spiritually. He completely heals him! This man lacks nothing at this moment. It would have been easier for Jesus to say your sins are forgiven because no one can test or see that. Yet, after that, He says, walk! This is the palpable miracle that everyone sees, and Scripture says because of it, they were all amazed and glorified God. The physical healing was apparent, but that doesn't mean it was more or less important than the man's spiritual healing. As followers of Christ, we are to eradicate sin, bondage, and physical illness in Jesus's name!

Another example is in Acts 3, where Peter and John encounter a lame man. He was lame from birth. In Acts 3:6, Peter commands the man to walk in the name of Jesus, and immediately, He does! But here's the kicker: He does not just walk. Verse 8 explains that after the healing, the man walks, leaps, and praises God! I love this because it is Jesus working through Peter, providing an example of what it can look like for us today as disciples, but also because he is healed physically (walking), emotionally (leaping), and spiritually (praising)! When Jesus and we as followers perform miracles in Jesus's name, the healings are sozo. It's spirit, soul, and body! Hallelujah!

I include these examples because Jesus still heals trauma today! We are walking, leaping, and praising examples. While the world's systems may be helpful at times, and God can certainly use them, nothing can replace an encounter with Jesus. If I could give any advice to someone like me who has dealt with trauma, it's this:

1. Get an encounter with the Lord Jesus,
2. Ask Him to bring complete healing and wholeness to the places that are traumatized.
3. Sit with the Holy Spirit and ask Him where the trauma came from.

He is gentle. If you allow Him, He'll take you back to the darkest places and show you that He was always with you. Even though He didn't cause the pain, He will most certainly redeem it and restore you!

(If you have trouble experiencing this alone, I urge you to check out SOZO ministry. You can find places to go in person or even engage in guided SOZO ministry online at www.bethelsozo.com. We have had SOZO sessions in our deepest seasons of grief, and we had some of the most powerful healing encounters with Jesus that I can remember.)

Reflection:

~ Is there any trauma that you are still dealing with and need freedom from?

Prayer:

Father God, I come before You, knowing You are our healer and freedom giver. I ask for healing of soul wounds, protection, and breaking off of shame. I choose to forgive people and situations that may have caused me trauma (be as specific as you possibly can here). I repent for not recognizing it sooner and ask that You walk me through freedom. I do not allow any more trauma or fear to control my life. I surrender to Your love, Lord, and receive Your healing in Jesus's name. Amen.

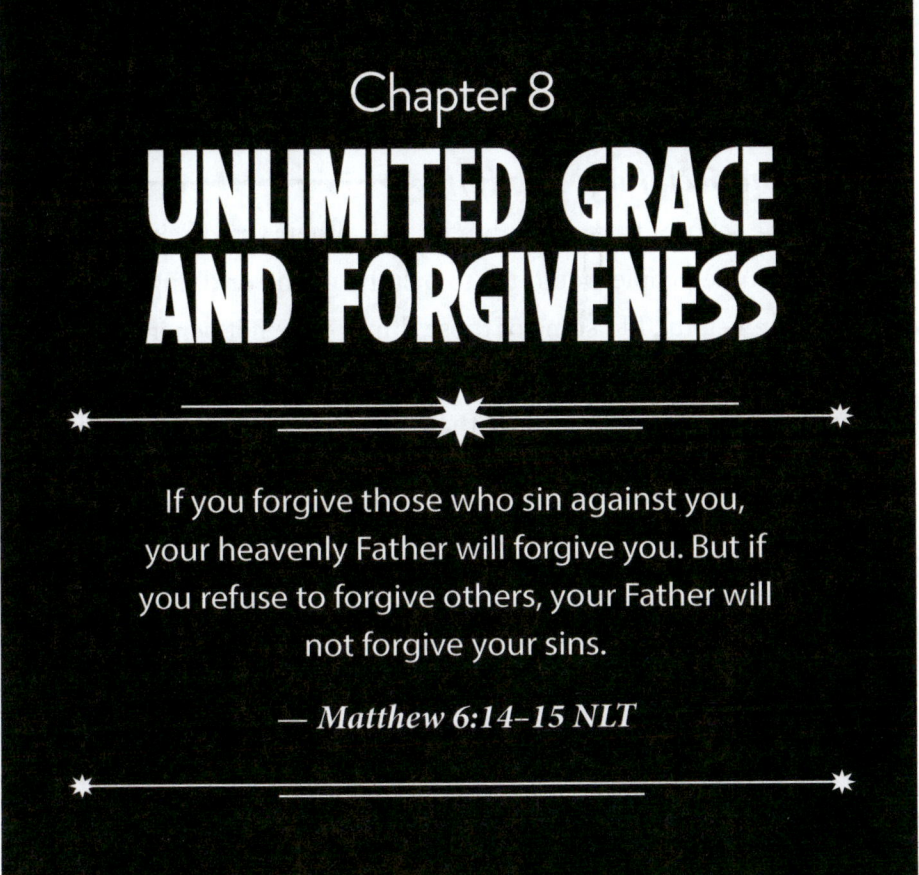

Chapter 8

UNLIMITED GRACE AND FORGIVENESS

If you forgive those who sin against you,
your heavenly Father will forgive you. But if
you refuse to forgive others, your Father will
not forgive your sins.

— Matthew 6:14–15 NLT

Time doesn't heal every wound. Cleansing does. Wounds represent the pain we have experienced, and when someone says something painful or hurtful to us, it feels like salt in the wound. In our season of immense pain, many people said words that deeply hurt. Some people's actions brought pain, anger, or sadness to our journey. People would say things like:

"God must have just had better plans."

"I guess it was God's will."

"Don't worry, you are still so young."

"Have you thought about adoption?"

We understand what some of these people were trying to say and that their intent was not to hurt us. However, they did not understand our situation and, unfortunately, did not think before they spoke. We had to learn to have unlimited grace for all of it. We had to learn to forgive.

Hurtful and Helpful (Melody) ✳━━━━━━━━

Some chose to say nothing, and others made inflammatory comments. Some people would try to help by giving or doing things they thought were helpful, but some of those things were not beneficial to us in those early days. Others took the time to ask what we would like or how they could help instead of pushing their way in, even if it was a meal that fit our preferences. Sometimes, we didn't know what we needed or wanted.

I remember a moment when some people we knew had a private meeting together and expressed to David how they thought I wasn't letting anyone in. They had never expressed that to me personally or even thought about how vulnerable that would be for me. They complained and became victims themselves. No one took the time to ask and let me know how they felt. It seemed so touchy for everyone, and no one wanted to ask the uncomfortable questions. I'm so thankful I had some friends who asked uncomfortable questions while giving their support, and I appreciated it so much. Their honesty in admitting that they didn't know the right thing to do was refreshing.

We had to learn to forgive many people and get to the point where we could pray for them and blessings in their lives. That didn't happen overnight, though, and it wasn't easy. I realized I had been hard on myself. I had not truly loved the person God had made me to be because of it. Constantly comparing myself or our situation to others only brought bitterness and hurt.

The Release of Forgiveness (Melody) ✳━━━━━━━━

I went through an intense physical and emotional healing time the summer after Kanaan's passing. I was in South Carolina with David, doing treatments for high levels of mold found in my body. I remember feeling like life wasn't fair, and I couldn't understand why I was dealing with this on top of everything else. But God was doing something more significant than we realized. God had so much grace for me during that time. I ended up reading through a book on forgiveness, and it was life-changing for me. I remember opening the book with a thump in my chest, knowing it was time to start letting go. Healing and forgiveness go hand in hand. I chose to forgive every person in my life who had ever said or done something offensive or hurtful (whether they realized it or not) so I could finally receive some healing. I took a journal and wrote down every person throughout my life up to this time that I had not forgiven completely. I had forgotten about some of those people, or I just never had processed the hurt. The hurt maybe didn't seem like a big deal anymore, but under the surface, it was. It oddly had become a comfort to me and kept me in a victim mindset. I went through a journey of releasing the bitterness, hurt, shame, jealousy, and envy I had been holding onto.

You may have heard it said that to forgive someone fully, you should be able to pray for blessing in that person's life. To be transparent, I was not there yet with some people in my life. I needed to go through each person in my journal and forgive and release each one from my heart prison. There were a lot of captives released that week! Most of all, I had to forgive myself, the biggest prisoner of all.

While learning in depth about forgiveness, I knew I would need to continue forgiving certain people in my life who were like sandpaper to me. There were people who would continue to bring on offenses, whether intentionally or not, and I would need to continue to make a conscious choice to release them. I remember so many times stressing myself out and getting sick because of the swirling drama and offenses. It ruined and wasted many nights in our marriage. It prevented us from gaining freedom in some situations. It caused us to isolate because we couldn't handle being around certain people.

When you go through a painful season or trial in your life, the enemy knows you are more susceptible to being offended and hurt by people. Pushing back bitterness is a choice that must be made every day, despite how others treat you or your family. Forgiveness destroys a victim mentality. You become an overcomer when you forgive. If you can become like Jesus through this, you win! We cannot control other people's behavior or what they say, but we can control our own.

When it comes to bitterness and unforgiveness, something is usually tormenting us. It could be lies that the enemy is spoon-feeding us, trauma, pain, hurtful words from other people, bad habits, sickness, or comparison. As a person of justice, at times, it felt fair not to forgive until that person would apologize. But that's never what Christ did. We must lay down our justice wants and let God bring that in His timing. To walk through forgiveness for people who would never apologize for offenses, hurtful words, or actions seemed unfair. But bitterness breeds the feeling of "it's not fair." It breeds jealousy and comparison. Sometimes, we find ourselves trying to collect something from someone who can't pay us. We have to get to the spot where we can forgive others, knowing they may never ask for forgiveness from us. It's a hard pill to swallow at first, but it's necessary for our healing and freedom. *In relationships, there will always be opportunities for offense, but never allow a disagreement or hurt to rule your love for that person.*

Forgive as Christ Forgave (Melody) ✴━━━━━━━━━━

This brings me to a time when God gave us a test when we could choose how to act regardless of how painful the situation was. We had received a note from someone we knew well who was pregnant. Now, if I put myself into her shoes, I'm sure she felt like she didn't know how to share the news face-to-face or didn't know what to do, so she wrote instead. It was during a Vikings game, which turned into a loss, so David was already dealing with disappointment that night. Yes, I know it's just a game, but to him, it's more. Later, we opened the Christmas card given to us and found the note. We immediately started tearing up. Yet another couple was pregnant instead of us—again. And it was someone we knew we would see many times during the pregnancy. We were happy for the couple but sad for us. We were sad to realize we were the last to find out. It was a constant battle in our minds, but we had a choice that night. We could sulk in our sadness or choose to love and rejoice with them. The internal struggle began. My heart hurt and felt like it was going to burst, so my mind tried to protect me by telling me not to go or say anything. I froze.

In this case, not saying anything would not be the right thing to do. We prayed and asked God to be with us and help us communicate that we loved them even though it was tough. The next day, we met with them to rejoice and pray over them. We loved them as Jesus would instead of isolating ourselves. Sure, it was hard, but a new life from God was growing, which was to be honored and celebrated. We had to adjust our attitudes many times despite the way we were approached (or avoided). Just like the Israelites, we need to be reminded that our attitude in the wilderness determines how long we will stay there! We wanted to get out of the wilderness, so we had to choose to be like Jesus!

Forgiving a rude customer or person cutting in front of you may come quickly, but forgiving someone who has wounded, abused, offended, hurt, or said piercing words to you can be difficult. So, what does it mean to forgive? Our English word forgive stems from the Greek verb aphiemi, which means "to let go."[20] To hold something against another is unforgiveness; to let it go is to forgive. In God's deep love for us, He lets our offenses go. I love what theologian Miroslav Volf says, "To forgive is to condemn the fault but to spare the doer."[21]

20

Chapter Eight

"Aphiemi," Bible Study Tools, accessed February 6, 2025, https://www.biblestudytools.com/lexicons/greek/nas/aphiemi.html.
[21] Miroslav Volf, *Free of Charge: Giving and Forgiving in a Culture Stripped of Grace* (Grand Rapids: Zondervan, 2005), 141.

Amid forgiveness, I was constantly reminded of God's grace. Grace is undeserved favor. Grace cannot be earned; it is something that God freely gives. We had to do that very same thing to others. We all are to give grace even if it feels undeserved. As a person grieving, it seems odd and wrong to have to be the one to give grace, but it's the example that Christ gave us. "Be kind and compassionate to one another, forgiving each other, just as in Christ God forgave you" (Eph. 4:32). Giving grace to someone is a choice. It's a choice to forgive someone. We always have a decision because of the free will Christ gives us. We also have the option to give grace to ourselves. We do not always get it right! Sometimes, we have inflicted hurt and pain onto others without knowing. Sometimes, we are our own worst enemy. The Bible tells us we need to love our neighbors as ourselves. We can condemn ourselves for not forgiving or repenting sooner for how we have acted, but we must lay that down before the Lord too. He is always ready and willing to forgive.

Complete Forgiveness (Melody) ✳━━━━━━━━━━━━

Some of the symptoms I encountered early on in our journey of forgiveness were isolation, mistrusting people, misreading actions, insecurity, loneliness, lack of peace, and anxiety. Just because you experience some of this does not mean you have unforgiveness in your heart. You know if you do or not. These are just some of the examples of how it can affect you. For some people, even sickness can come as a result of unforgiveness. For us, this was not necessarily the case. I went on to deal with other health issues despite forgiving people in my life. I had to go deeper with God, put my faith into action, and trust in His promises despite what was happening around me.

We learned to forgive many times, and through the following months and years, we would need to continue exercising that with specific people. What we wanted was lasting forgiveness. It couldn't be temporary or halfway. We needed complete forgiveness so we could experience freedom:

no keeping score and no keeping tabs on what someone had done. God's commandment on this is vital. God expects us to model forgiveness after Him. Matthew 6:14–15 (NLT) highlights this: "If you forgive those who sin against you, your heavenly Father will forgive you. But if you refuse to forgive others, your Father will not forgive your sins."

God doesn't torture us, but He allows us to be tortured by others when we do not forgive. When there is unforgiveness in your life, you will have something negative show up. There are always consequences when we do not forgive. You are living a lie if you think that forgetting, pushing it down, or hiding it won't bring some suffering in your life. It's like living with an open wound that you try to cover up, medicate, ignore, or pick at. We have to get to the spot where we decide that we are going to let that wound air out, go to the hospital, and heal.

God doesn't punish us; He disciplines us. He wants us to learn to forgive so we don't have to experience any suffering from unforgiveness. Trust me, you do not want to hold any debts in your heart. When you take that step of forgiveness, the torment is canceled! Forgiving others helps you to not undergo painful discipline for it. In Matthew 18, Jesus shares a story about forgiving debts (sins). The king in the story had compassion for his servant and forgave his debt, letting it all go. That man who was forgiven then demanded another servant to pay a debt he owed. When the servant couldn't pay, the man had him thrown into prison. When the king found out, he had the unmerciful servant put into prison and tortured. Jesus told this story to get us to understand that we need to have that same compassion to forgive others who have debts against us.

With great mercy, God spreads His compassion on us like a cloak and lovingly cancels our debts. He does not ignore or overlook our offenses but does not hold them against us. Since we all sin and cause damage to God's creation, we each owe a great debt for it. God is ready and willing to forgive us if we repent! He has already made the way through Jesus. That's the first step!

But when we do not have forgiveness in our hearts, we can't have true inner peace. God removes the peace as a discipline until we forgive. Think of it this way. We receive some torment from the enemy when we do not forgive, but if we reject Christ and are not born again, we are tormented forever after we die. Approaching relationships with an unforgiving attitude proposes we haven't opened ourselves up to receive God's forgiveness. If we've received the forgiveness that is available because of the cross, we can learn to extend grace to others. Here's an example:

✳ Deep hurts and offenses usually require about a year to be able to forgive from your heart. We grant verbal forgiveness because we know the Bible tells us we have to. But most [of the] time we still hold resentment and judgments against the person in our heart. If we respond to God's dealings with us, we then grant forgiveness from our soul and then finally we pull upon enough grace to forgive from our heart. Just verbal and soul forgiveness will not suffice. When we finally forgive from the heart it [is] as though it happened to another person, we release all anger, resentment and judgments against the person and when we meet them we can look them in the eye and say God bless you and mean it from our heart. It does not make what they did to us right but it does make us right with God and clears things where God can . . . restore us back to a place of trust and fellowship with God."[22]

A softening of our hearts is what we need in the act of forgiveness. It's choosing to be the bigger person. When we don't grant forgiveness, the infection in our hearts spreads. We know unforgiveness has taken root when we are rigid with resentment or bitterness. It's time to take out unforgiveness, root and all. You've maybe heard the saying, "Resentment

[22] Bill Hamon, *How Can These Things Be?: A Preacher and a Miracle Worker But Denied Heaven!* (Destiny Image Incorporated, 2015), 42–43.

is like drinking poison and waiting for the other person to die." It ends up destroying us and entangles us in a prison. It's in these moments that we need to wrestle with God until we feel able to forgive. It can be a long process of letting go while God slowly heals our scars and wounds. You might need someone to walk alongside you, like a trusted counselor, friend, or mentor so you can work through the pain. We learned to be more patient with people, less reactive to drama, more understanding of people affecting us negatively, and calmly work through conflict.

If you have been in a toxic situation, it does not at all mean that you have to trust that person again. You can love and forgive them as Christ does, but it does not mean you need to give them permission to hurt you again. Continue practicing giving it to God—each day, each moment. I went through this time and time again. I had verbally forgiven someone and couldn't figure out why that person still bothered me. I realized I couldn't change anyone and needed to accept other people's flaws because I had many too! This allowed me to navigate relational hurt and be empowered to follow the ways of Jesus.

Exposing Lies (David)

Amidst all the pain, confusion, and hurt, there were and still are many opportunities to harbor unforgiveness. In many ways, by the world's standards, it is wholly justified. To protect privacy and relationships, I want to refrain from sharing many specific examples publicly, but some of the things that were said and done to us during our grieving journey were nothing short of horrendous. They were insensitive at best and, at worst, downright destructive, manipulative, and malicious. It was one of the most complex parts of the grief journey. If you've ever gone through it, you know that you watch people return to their routine, and they slowly forget about and stop talking about, in our case, our kids. That hurts in and of itself, but then those same people turn around and try to advise you on how to "get over it" or "move on."

People that I love and trust the most to this day said stuff like that to me. Let me set the record straight. I'm never going to "get over" losing my children. I don't even desire to. I'm not going to move on. What we choose to do and what we are doing with the Lord's help is to grow around the grief and to move forward. We are turning our pain into purpose even as we write these words to hopefully bring breakthroughs and hope into your life and situation. We want to honor our children's legacy by glorifying God and helping others. I hope the "Land of Kanaan" gets more beautiful and anointed with every passing year. I want our children's lives to become memorial stones to remind us and others that God can still turn ashes into beauty and that He still does turn graves into gardens! I want to embrace the pain and hurt with Jesus because, quite frankly, He's the only one who truly gets it and me and all the nuances that go with it.

Through it all, I've learned an essential truth: The enemy uses these tragedies to create division and dysfunction. Satan tries to cloud my thinking, and he tries to convince me that my loved ones are trying to hurt me by their words and actions. And while it's okay and necessary to acknowledge that their actions and words hurt and work through that, it's equally necessary for our healing to forgive and move forward. By worldly standards, we have every right to hold a grudge, get bitter, get angry, and hold on to resentment and unforgiveness. If I told you each story, your human side would justify the hurt and bitterness along with me. Here's the kicker: I genuinely want to give my all to follow Jesus. If I want to follow Jesus, forgiveness isn't an option but a requirement. I know the world's systems say it's okay and even justified for me to hold onto things, but if I want sozo healing, as we discussed in the previous chapter, I must learn to let go and release people.

The first step in all this is realizing when you are believing a lie or a partial truth. For example, it's excruciating when relatives or friends forget to acknowledge that they have a grandson, sibling, cousin, or friend! We witnessed people in our lives fail to acknowledge our children when they talked about their family or relationships. In those vulnerable moments, the enemy swoops in and feeds Melody and me lies like, "They don't care. They forgot. Kanaan is out of sight and out of mind," or any other kind of fill-in-the-blank garbage along those lines. The first step in forgiveness and unlimited grace is realizing that the source of those thoughts is not rooted in reality; it is rooted in lies. In these moments, pause before you let yourself go into a tailspin! Sometimes, I have to say out loud, "Holy Spirit, I know that's a lie; what is the truth about this moment?" Many times, right then and there, He'll softly speak to me something like, "They do care; they just are uncomfortable and don't know how to process it. They even thought of Kanaan in their answer but were afraid to say it because they didn't want this conversation to turn into a downer."

Our society needs to do grief better. We like to bury it, numb it, or mask it. We can't pick and choose when we acknowledge life and when we don't. If we believe that life begins at conception, we can't ignore our brothers and sisters in Heaven who only lived in the womb or for a short time in the NICU. It hurts our hearts as parents who have lost children, but more importantly, it dishonors the life that God miraculously brought. I'm not trying to tell you how to do it. Everyone responds and honors differently. Don't miss opportunities to honor every life.

Let me gently remind you that ***any thought you have that doesn't produce hope is probably rooted in a lie***. I had to realize that any idea that made me think less of myself, God, or others was a lie. In this process, we must take all our thoughts captive and ask the Holy Spirit what the truth is. We often have to create declarations from the truths we hear and speak them aloud until the lie begins to fade.

We must face the hard truth in these seasons that even if some don't apologize, it's still our cross to bear to forgive. People often don't realize that they hurt you, and you must have some grace for that. Forgiveness sets us free and aligns our thoughts with the thoughts of Jesus. The Bible says that we have the mind of Christ (1 Cor. 2:16), which means we have the ability to think like Him. The way He sees people and even hurtful situations is always through the lens of forgiveness and reconciliation. We can only honestly do it as we lean on Him for comfort and guidance.

Jesus Is Enough (David) ✳————————————————————

If you've been a believer for any amount of time, you've probably heard the story of Jesus calming the storm in Mark 4. I want to point out a nuance in this story. The disciples and Jesus are in a boat at sea, and there's a terrible storm. The disciples were fishermen, and they knew the severity of this and began to panic. The ironic part is that Jesus is sleeping through all of this. It finally gets to the point where the panic is too much. The disciples wake up Jesus and inform Him of the matter. He sternly rebukes the waves and wind, and the storm stops immediately. It's a complete miracle, and the disciples are astonished, but Jesus seems a little angry that they woke Him from His nap! He asks them if they have any faith. If I'm at liberty to read between the lines with the Holy Spirit here, I believe Jesus is surprised by their lack of faith. He realizes that they still need Him to do something, to perform miracles, and to calm the storm for them to feel good. They weren't at the point yet where the presence of Jesus was enough.

To achieve absolute forgiveness, the presence of Jesus has to be enough. In a perfect world, it shouldn't matter if He changes the situation or the person apologizes. What matters is our ability to see Jesus in all situations and follow Him in forgiveness.

Theologian Desmond Tutu explains, "Forgiveness does not mean condoning what has been done. It means taking what happened seriously and not minimizing it; drawing out the sting in the memory that threatens to poison our entire existence."[23] The closer the emotional or relational tie you had with a person who hurt you, the broader and deeper the wound will be.

---

[23] Desmond Tutu, No Future Without Forgiveness (Random House, 2012), 271.

How does an infection in your heart start? First, unforgiveness, then anger, bitterness, slander, and resentment, which can sometimes lead to hatred and vengeance. You might get ill or have negative feelings toward someone; you may replay the instance or words in your mind. Then you lose your peace; you withdraw when around them, you misread motives or actions because of distrust, you talk about someone else in the worst light, you keep score or a hidden list of actions or words directed at you or others, you decide it's okay to dislike them, you avoid them because you can't stand them, and or you want to get even with that person. These all grieve the Holy Spirit. We have to forgive and repent for these habits and ways.

How long do you want to stay there? A sick heart transforms us into someone we don't like. If you are not careful, it can become engraved into your personality. Lies from the enemy try to divert you from forgiveness because he knows you will be set free. Forgiveness is all about our part! It's about us getting freedom and peace. The person we choose to forgive may never decide to do the same, so they live a life of hopelessness, pain, and defeat. You can't change what happened or go back in time and reverse the hurt. Choose to walk in repentance and forgiveness so you can live a life of peace. You might think, "I don't even want a relationship with that person, so what's the point of forgiving?" It's a big point. It will heal your past with that person; the future, however, is another issue. It's not your job to worry about that! People change, forgive, and repent. We never know what God could be doing in that person's life. We have to live in a way that calls out the good or what could be and how God sees them despite how they live.

Habits of Forgiveness (Melody) ✴━━━━━━━━━━━━━━━━━

I love what Bruce Wilkinson says: "Forgiveness releases the torment from the past but does not require any kind of future relationship."[24] You are not signing up to be best friends with that person; you are simply letting

---

[24]Bruce Wilkinson and Mark E. Strong, The Secret of Lasting Forgiveness: How to Find Peace by Forgiving Others and Yourself (Zeal Books, 2018), 67–68.

them go from your heart prison, bringing freedom to your entire being. Any pain or wound in your life took something away and caused you profound loss, but you can't wait for things to be fixed before you choose to forgive! You may need to put up safeguards. You may not be able to share personal or vulnerable things with that person anymore, and that's okay. You have to choose how your relationships will look. There has to be an element of asking the Lord to help guard your heart while at the same time not shutting out every single person. We all have different layers of relationships. Some people are close to you, while others are distant. It doesn't make it necessarily bad or good. Remember that person may never come to you and repent, but God requires you to forgive every time. That includes not counting how many times you forgive them. No keeping score! God never keeps us bound but releases us and then forgives us. Extend compassion to the person themselves, not only what they did or said.

If you know you must let go of bitterness and offenses, here is an easy place to start. Grab a journal, as I did, and write the names of people you feel bitterness, envy, judgment, or anger toward. Now, write down the things they said or did directly to you or even things others have said that they said (sometimes unknowingly, which also causes us harm). Don't leave details out; it's essential to recognize what has caused you pain so you can release it. Ask the Lord to help soften your heart. Imagine letting them go from your heart prison one by one. You release them, and now you can forgive them. Pray a prayer of forgiveness for each person and situation. When you cannot think of anything anymore, ask the Holy Spirit to reveal anything else you may have forgotten that needs to be released. Pray and ask the Lord to help you love them as He does and to bless them as in Matthew 5:44–45: "But I tell you, love your enemies and pray for those who persecute you, that you may be children of your Father in heaven. He causes his sun to rise on the evil and the good, and sends rain on the righteous and the unrighteous."

This can take time to walk through all these steps, and that's okay.

God has grace for you. When you can pray for blessing upon them, it's like putting a seal on an envelope. You have finally dealt with your unforgiveness. You are meant to be free in every area of your life! When you build walls to protect yourself from pain, you also exclude yourself from lasting joy in your heart. Here's the hope in all of this: Bad habits of unforgiveness can be replaced with good ones! Get into the habit of having compassion, not accepting negativity, giving grace, and being who God made you to be. Use your journal to mark down days of significant forgiveness. Watch how God begins to change you and your life through it. Don't let unforgiveness block your destiny! If you find yourself in a situation that needs true reconciliation, be the one to offer forgiveness first. Since we cannot cover it in this book, it simply boils down to offering forgiveness and the offender receiving that. The offender must acknowledge wrongdoing and work to repair what has been broken.

When Am I Done Forgiving? (David)

Sometimes, it was hard for us to tell if we'd forgiven a person entirely or if there was something that we were still holding onto in our hearts. The enemy loves to suggest that forgiveness hasn't happened and/or will never happen! We have to recognize that this is a lie because forgiveness is possible. It's possible because of the life of Christ. He modeled it, and the same spirit that raised Him from the dead lives in us! That is the key. You know you've forgiven the day you can think about that person, look at them, and pray a sincere blessing over them. Sometimes, you must fake it until you make it, which is perfectly okay. It can take some time for our mind, spirit, and body to connect and all be in sync. If you have second thoughts, partner with the Holy Spirit to bless them and prophesy a God-ordained future over them. Call out the gold in them that God put in each person. That's the moment when forgiveness becomes fruitful.

There can be times when our human nature wants to get back at people or even keep score. In these moments, we must remind ourselves that it's not our job. Jesus is going to vindicate you at the restoration of all things. Rest in that. You don't have to do it yourself. Vindication is the Lord's. Remember that forgiveness can be a process; learn to surrender every moment to that process. Eventually, seemingly suddenly, there will be a breakthrough!

Reflection:

~ Is there anyone that you need to forgive and give grace to?

~ What does it look like to give grace to that person?

Prayer:

Lord, show me if there is anyone I need to forgive today, including myself. Reveal areas that I need to accept Your grace and give it to others. I repent of not forgiving sooner and ask for forgiveness. Help me forgive those who have hurt me. Guide me as I work through each relationship. In Jesus's name, I pray. Amen.

Chapter 9

BETWEEN THE PROMISE AND THE FULFILLMENT

---✳---

"For my thoughts are not your thoughts,
neither are your ways my ways," declares the
Lord. "As the heavens are higher than the
earth, so are my ways higher than your ways
and my thoughts than your thoughts."

— Isaiah 55:8–9

There are moments in life when you struggle to believe what God said, but you press on. These moments are the tension in the journey. The journey matters most to God, not necessarily the fulfillment of the promise, although that brings Him glory! The journey is where the blood, sweat, and tears are spent. You might find yourself, as we did many times, praying desperate prayers, spending time in worship, seeking God, crying in confusion, and finally surrendering all you have left. Be relentless with your cries of hope. When you are so close to a breakthrough, something usually happens that will test you. It's a test of your faith and your obedience. The enemy wants us to question and doubt what God said. He wants us to second guess if we heard God right and to come into agreement with the liar's negativity. Maybe you are thinking, "I've taken steps of obedience, but it didn't turn out how I thought it would. Does walking in obedience even make a difference?"

We walked through a season like that. We had many words from God declaring that we would have children. There was no denying what God had said. We stood by His word and continued to believe He would remain faithful in bringing it to pass. He had spoken, and we had listened, so we decided to move forward. When you receive a word from God—whether through Scripture, His still small voice, a prophetic word, a dream, or a picture in your mind that keeps coming up—God knows that you will need the reminder to keep going forward. He knows you will need the nourishment of His words to persevere. Be gripped by God's promises even more than the pain of your disappointment.

Surrender Control (Melody) ✳━━━━━━━━━━━━

After taking time to do some healing and processing after Kanaan's loss, in November 2022, we started the process of adoption. It had taken some time for us to pray and be open to it, but we felt God's call. If you had asked us a year or two before, we wouldn't have thought we would be pursuing it, but God changed our hearts! Once we took the step, we felt peace. We didn't know how our family would grow and how God would bring His word to pass, so we decided to lay all options down and surrender them to Him. We knew our family would grow the way God wanted it to. We just had to be open and lay down our desires.

After doing all the intense paperwork, home study, fingerprints, background checks, making our profile book, sending applications to various attorneys and agencies, and paying multiple fees, we were finally active for domestic infant adoption at the end of January 2023. We had no idea what we were getting into, but we trusted God and laid down our preconceived notions of how it would happen. In February, we started getting cases brought to our attention. It seemed like a whirlwind sometimes. If you are unfamiliar with adoption, sometimes, you only have twenty-four hours or less to decide on a case. That was hard for us. Each agency and attorney worked differently, so we went with a multi-faceted approach to get more cases. Each agency had an "at-risk" fee. This meant that in infant adoption, there are many expenses the adoptive parents potentially pay for. Any of the following can be included in an at-risk fee: transportation, food, phone, living, pregnancy care, clothes, agency fees, state fees, and more.

We were pursuing an infant adoption, preferably at birth because we wanted to have that opportunity to bond right away. It was hard to say no to some circumstances, but if we didn't feel peace or good about it, we had to wait on God. There were many times we said yes, but the birth mom ended up picking another family. Those were challenging moments, but we were able to process them quickly and remain optimistic about the next one. In late June of 2023, we got a call one day from an agency we had not gotten a case from yet. When we answered the phone, they told us that a birth mom had chosen us! The emotion that came was a different feeling because, in all the previous cases, we had to say if we wanted to be considered by a birth mom and her situation or not. This time, a birth mom had already picked us, so all that was on the line was our answer!

They proceeded to tell us that this mother was going to be having her baby the very next week and that we would need to fly down to Florida to meet her the day before her c-section. In short, we ended up saying yes hours later. It was a whirlwind! We were so excited! We were in the middle of finishing our new house, but that now went on the back burner. It was time to go meet our baby. We packed our bags as fast as we could, with our hearts racing. We booked our flights and rental car, packed all the baby stuff, and headed out the next day. We told our families, who were joyful with us and held us in prayer and support. I remember thinking on the plane how much this trip could change our lives forever. As David and I gripped each other's hands on the plane, we prayed.

I was nervous to meet the birth mom but also excited to see her personality and give her our love, honor, and support. The next day, we were to have lunch with the adoption agent and the birth mom. We met at a restaurant of her choice and brought her a gift. When we walked in and sat down, we could tell she was extremely nervous and shy. We were anxious and excited. She was a young mom with no resources or support. We listened to her story (as much as she would tell us) and asked questions about her and what she liked. Trying to get to know someone in two hours is impossible for anyone, let alone in a situation as unique as this, with all the emotions swirling. By the end of the conversation, we exchanged contact information to support her in any way she needed. We knew she could change her mind at any moment, but we held onto hope that this was the child that God would bring into our lives to raise and love. We left that lunch hopeful and excited for the baby that would be born the next day! We went to get a few last essential items and some baby clothes.

The next day, the birth mom would be going to the hospital. We had one day to prepare before the baby was born. I became overwhelmed with so many details to think about. I knew, however, that I had to be strong because we didn't know for sure what would happen. There had been no birth plan discussed, so we were left in limbo; everything was out of our control. Relinquishing control is probably one of the hardest things for a human being. We wanted to know some kind of outcome so we could be prepared. It's in our human nature. In adoption, there typically is no room for that. You must choose to surrender and believe that God will be with you no matter the result. We prayed and worshiped as we prepared what we could.

The next day, we waited to hear from the agency or birth mom that the baby had been born. We did not know the gender, which would be a sweet surprise! Many hours passed, and still, we had not heard anything. We began to get a little concerned and contacted our agent. She explained to us that the birth mom's c-section got delayed and happened later than expected. She was planning to be in the room with the birth mom, but she asked her to leave, so she didn't know any more than we did. That was nerve-wracking for me!

A couple more hours later, we finally heard from the birth mom. She was recovering from surgery, and she said we could come to the hospital to meet the baby. We let our agent know, and she had us go by ourselves to the hospital. It was such an interesting experience. Nothing was what I expected.

As we entered the quiet and dim room, we congratulated her and brought her favorite yellow flowers. We saw a beautiful baby girl. She was so precious. She was perfect! We got to spend some time with her that night, holding her, and then eventually, the birth mom asked us to leave and come back the next day so she could get some rest. We felt better after getting to meet our future daughter that night. We were excited and nervous at the same time! It would only be another day (or so we thought) that this birth mom would officially make her decision.

Up to this point, she was choosing us to parent her child, and she had not changed her mind yet. The next day, our agent let us know that because of the c-section, they were letting her take another day before she had to make her decision and sign papers because of discharge timing. This extra day typically is not given in this particular state (at the time of writing this book); birth moms have forty-eight hours, and then they must either sign papers or change their minds.

Again, we waited and prayed. The wait felt like forever. We thanked God and asked Him to protect and be with us. We couldn't do anything because we needed to be ready to go to the hospital at any point. We sent her messages but heard nothing for almost the whole day until evening again. She explained later that she had friends and co-workers who were visiting. Again, it made me nervous that she was possibly changing her mind. If she was changing her mind, I wanted the bandage to be ripped off right away so we could go home and process it instead of being pulled along.

But we held onto hope, and our agent reassured us that her situation was not healthy for this child, so she didn't think she would change her mind. However, there was still a chance she would. The next morning came, and we got to go back briefly to see the baby.

The hospital was small, and the rooms were intimate, so we never got complete private time with the baby when we visited, which was hard for all of us. I can't imagine the birth mom watching us smile and love on that baby. It must have been so hard as she battled with her decision. At the same time, we had given a lot just to be there: time away from work, finances, and our hearts.

Unfortunately, this story did not end as we had hoped. In the last hours, the birth mom changed her mind. I remember our agent crying with us as she felt so bad, but she was also concerned because she didn't know how this mother would raise her child. She didn't have support, money, baby supplies, or even a car seat.

It was hard for us to swallow. We had vulnerably put our hearts out there and shared our story, only to be shut out. Let me take a moment to say this. In the realm of adoption, the decision a birth mom or birth parents make is incredibly hard and painful. It is hard for the adoptive parents as well. Many couples like ourselves had already experienced many losses or maybe never were able to get pregnant and ended up getting disappointed again. It's hard for everyone involved. There has to be so much grace, so much love, and so much honor.

When a mother decides to parent her child, it's beautiful, and it is the original God-intended design, yet it is hard for adoptive parents who have waited for a child. The reality is that someone will end up giving up a child, and someone else will end up parenting that child. We had to walk away and fly home with empty arms. When we arrived home, we couldn't believe what had just happened. Our emotions and circumstances were in a tailspin in such a short time.

Emotional Rollercoaster (Melody) *━━━━━━━━━━━━*

We took a couple of weeks off before considering getting active with our agencies again. We wanted to take time to pray and process together. After those two weeks, we decided to get active, and at the end of July, we received another phone call.

"A birth mom has chosen you!" the agent exclaimed over the phone.

We were again shocked with potential excitement while guarding our hearts a little more. They gave us an entire day to decide. We read through this mother's information and talked to the consultant we were working with. She gave us her advice and opinion and thought it was low risk.

We prayed and talked through it more together and felt nothing. We didn't feel peace about saying yes or no. It was an odd feeling. Typically, in our lives, we follow peace. This time, God seemed to watch how we would respond if He didn't give us direction. We decided to take a step of faith. This baby would not be born for four months, so it would give us time to connect, support, and get to know the birth mom and create a relationship. We met on Zoom the next week and met this beautiful birth mom. She had a boyfriend, which made the situation a little more interesting, but he was all in with the adoption.

In August, we flew to meet her and started developing a relationship with her. We would message back and forth and stay connected to our adoption agent to get updates when they were available. Things were going well, so we prepared a baby suitcase and made plans. Fast forward, it was now October, and it was getting close to the arrival time for the baby. We found out it was going to be a girl! The doctor had said they thought she might deliver early, so we got prepared. Then, in the middle of October, everything went silent. The birth mom stopped responding to us and the adoption agency: no answering calls, texts, or home visits.

Two weeks went by, and nothing. Unfortunately, our agency had to drop the case and take us off for our sake. They never heard from her again, and neither did we. It was tough. Our emotions went wild as we felt used, lied to, and disappointed again. This time, we were unsure if we would get active again with our agencies. It felt too risky, hard, emotionally draining, and financially straining. We had already lost thirty thousand dollars from the last two failed adoptions, and our savings were drained. At this point, we were unsure how to move forward or if we should.

No Second-Class Miracles (David) ✳━━━━━━━━━━━━

It was breathtaking. I felt as if I was walking in the garden of Eden. The colors were vibrant, and the smells were magnificent! I was by myself, but the presence of the Holy Spirit was palpable. I felt peace and joy, and it was as if I could reach out and hold onto them. There were fruit trees with lush fruit, gardens with delicious vegetables and flowers like I'd never seen before! As I walked along the banks of a crisp, refreshing, clear river, I saw mountains in the distance. As my five senses were overwhelmed with goodness, I felt emotions too! I was filled with hope—a renewed hope that breakthroughs and blessings were coming. I was speechless, and I couldn't tell where I was exactly. Was I in Heaven? Was it a national park of some sort? Just then, I felt the Holy Spirit nudge me to look up.

As I did, I noticed I was approaching a tall and gorgeous garden trellis. As I walked under the arbor, I saw giant, beautiful iguanas hanging from their tails, and their heads were almost touching mine. They were vibrant and emerald green. There were countless iguanas as far as I could see! I am not naturally a big reptile or lizard fan, but I didn't feel any fear or anxiousness at this moment. I felt awestruck by the beauty and filled with wonder.

For the first time in a while, I felt that I was looking forward to the future again and that the pain of the past had started to wither. As I looked again at all the iguanas, my alarm clock went off! It was a dream, but I immediately knew it was a dream from God. I felt peace and hope, like God was wrapping His enormous arms around me. So many elements of the dream were astounding, but the iguanas were the emphasis. I couldn't get the iguanas out of my head. We've learned much more since then, but I was not good at processing dreams with the Holy Spirit at the time, so naturally, I went to Google. I found lots of stuff—some good and some bad—but the thing that stuck out to me was fertility. Iguanas can symbolize fertility, so I filed it away as one more kiss from God amongst the others we received during the long and exhausting journey.

In our experience, God often gives us words, encouragement, and dreams because He knows we will need them.

The battle with infertility was getting long and daunting. We knew God was telling us to keep battling and fighting the good fight, but if we can be honest for the sake of transparency, it was not always easy to keep our hopes up. We had some fantastic friends and family who encouraged us to keep going, and we also had some who felt a bit more like Job's friends. They doubted and undermined the prophetic in our lives, and they probably thought they were helping by sharing what they thought was the truth. In reality, though, their doubts and questioning did rub in a hurtful way.

Not only did we have to hold onto hope for our dreams, but we felt we had to defend God, His words to us, and the fact that He still works in and through us supernaturally. The delay, disappointment, and doubt were taking their toll. Forgiveness and grace are necessary not just daily but even moment by moment.

Melody touched on this, but we had to come to a place of complete surrender. We had to come to a place of total obedience, no matter how crazy or impossible it seemed. We even had to give up our preferences and our right to understand things in order to align ourselves with total surrender.

As the disappointment, delay, and questioning began to set in again, we were at yet another crossroads. This one felt even more significant. We thought and believed that God would use natural health and wellness to bring about our miracle. We had learned so much and become much healthier (which we will share in more detail in the next chapter), but we still hadn't had a healthy baby, much less the healthy babies that were promised.

We thought God would give us a story and a ministry centered around supernatural healing. We thought He would use health and wellness as a career path because of the significant breakthroughs that were coming. That still might be true. I believe it is. However, at this moment, in the fall and early winter of 2022, we felt the call to lay it all down. We had to lay our dreams and ways of doing things on the altar. If only for a season, we had to give up our right to understand everything in order to get Heaven's peace in our situation and home.

For whatever reason, resorting to adoption or even more invasive medical procedures like IVF/IUI felt like a second-class miracle at the time. Part of us felt like we were giving up too soon, and the perception from the outside world was that once you begin the process of adoption, you've essentially resigned from the idea of having biological children. Let me take a moment to set the record straight for anyone who may be in the struggle and the questions. There are no second-class miracles! There are no second-class healings! God has, can, and still does use any means for His glory! That includes medical treatments, natural treatments, and supernatural healings. One does not necessarily glorify Him more than the other, and one does not necessarily require more faith than the other! The absolute key is discerning where God is in all of it and learning to hear His voice. God wants our hearts and our surrender. We had and have preferences about how the miracle would come about. We tend to be more natural and holistic-minded. We tend to press in and want to see more of the supernatural. All of that is awesome; there's nothing wrong with it! It becomes wrong when we worship the healing modality more than the healer. It's a heart issue that only we knew was going on. You can't see it from the outside necessarily.

So, as God spoke to and molded us, we laid it all down. We reached the breaking point again, where we came to a spot of total surrender. We felt God's stir leading us to adoption. We applied and got set up with agencies and home studies. We spent the money, time, resources, and energy getting our story and our family out there to potential birth mamas who wanted to pursue this courageous option. Adoption, for us, was not, and is not, resignation. I still believe that we will have multiple biological children and potentially more adopted ones too. I so much believe that maybe by the time this book hits the shelves, there will need to be edits because our process will have become the "suddenly" we have been praying for and hoping for so long!

A Touch from Heaven (David) ✳━━━━━━━━━━━━━━━

Adoption for us was surrender. It was obedience. It was coming to a spot where we didn't care as much about how God would grow our family; we just trusted that He would. We realized our story and purpose weren't just about us, our kids, and our family. We learned that mamas and babies out there needed to see Jesus's love shine through us in some pretty complex and desperate situations. Adoption was turning our pain into purpose. It was a way to live out our pro-life beliefs. It's one thing to post on social media about how horrific abortion is. It's totally different to stand up and be part of the solution. Adoption is near and dear to God's heart, so much so that He uses the language of adoption for all of us as His sons and daughters!

Now, it may be easy to assume that after this moment of surrender, things turned around for us. That's usually how the stories go, right? We had gone through so much hurt, pain, loss, and disappointment already. I know this act of surrender and obedience was a vital cog and a pivotal moment for us, but our reality didn't change immediately. Melody has already so elegantly shared the details of the adoption "interruptions," so I'll spare you from reading the same story twice. Still, I want to add some details from my perspective that add to the confusion and chaos we were experiencing.

During our trip down south to adopt (we thought to be) our baby girl, we weren't allowed to be in the hospital very much. We wanted to be there loving on who we thought would be our daughter, bonding, and loving on mama as much as possible. That's where our heart and passion were, but she wasn't our daughter yet, and we didn't have much say. We were left waiting with minimal details.

I remember our families and friends bombarding us with questions we couldn't answer. We weren't hiding anything. We simply didn't know many of the details. We like to find healing and recompense in nature. We spent what we thought would be our last moments as a family of two walking on the beach and exploring local national and state parks. It wasn't the stereotypical babymoon that people take nowadays, but we tried to make the most of it and get our minds off things the best we could.

I remember the moment like it was yesterday. It was another day in the blistering and humid heat. Our Minnesotan bodies couldn't handle much more. I turned the ignition off in the car and opened the door to explore a local park with Melody while we were hopeful for an invite to visit the hospital. I froze in my tracks. Although He wasn't, it was as if God was speaking audibly. There was a big, beautiful iguana in the parking lot just posing for me to see it. I realized that it wasn't just one but that this park was almost overrun with them. As we walked and prayed together, we saw families of iguanas at every turn. We felt God's peace as if I was back in the dream I described earlier.

I so desperately needed that touch from Heaven at that moment. Our God is so kind! Of course, I thought He would turn this specific situation around, but it was as if He didn't even need to. We knew then that God was in this adoption season no matter what happened. We had heard His voice, and we were obedient. Again, it was as if God knew what was about to happen to us (adoption interruption), and He gave us this experience so that we'd keep going.

Of course, as you already read, this situation was another disappointment for us. We couldn't believe it. And we faced another shortly after, in October of that same year. We were broken, scared, and reeling. Job's friends (if you will) started coming back. The questions didn't help: "Is the adoption agency legit? Do you have enough money to keep going? Did you pray before you said yes? Are you sure you heard God?"

It was hard and disappointing again. I'm sure some of it was due to our past that we maybe hadn't fully dealt with yet. Old wounds and trauma resurfaced. I was taken back to a moment that I had with God after the loss of our first daughter, Esther. That memory was all the way back to October of 2017, so six whole years had gone by, and there was still no healthy baby. I was processing the loss with the Holy Spirit on a walk in our woods. He spoke clearly at that moment and said, "I am redeeming the month of October. I AM!"

"That's great, God," I thought sarcastically. It sure doesn't feel like it. We've honored our babies in October for the last six years because October 15 is International Pregnancy and Infant Loss Day. As I was lamenting and complaining to God, He spoke again. "Put on your purple jersey," He said. He went on to explain (and I'm paraphrasing now) that the Vikings have hurt me time and time again, and they've never made it to the promised land (a Super Bowl championship)! Yet, every Sunday (or Thursday, Monday, or Saturday), I wear that purple jersey with renewed hope and passion. It's a silly example, I know, but realize that God speaks your language! It struck a chord with me. He was right. Why can I get my hopes up for a team I have no control over that has never won anything? Yet, getting my hopes up for the family God promised Melody and me is hard. So, for what it's worth, when it felt hopeless and when we felt lost, I responded with a prophetic act. I went into my closet and put on the purple jersey.

God's Ways, Not Ours (Melody) ✳

We had to relinquish control of our circumstances. Surrendering is hard. It's messy, tiring, scary, and risky. However, it's necessary. When we look at all the times in our journey when we didn't know what to do, we always had to surrender. We had to let go of control in our story. We had to let it be what God wanted. We reminded ourselves of the words that God had spoken. When you have a promise in your life, the enemy will always target what the Lord has spoken to you. There will be resistance from the enemy when the same word has been spoken over your life multiple times. I love Psalm 23:5, which says, "You prepare a table before me in the presence of my enemies. You anoint my head with oil; my cup overflows." The Lord prepares a table for us with nourishment for the journey. There, we can recognize His presence in the darkest and deepest valleys. We can feast on God's presence instead of the enemy's lies and negativity.

Throughout our journey, we often thought we had finally figured out what was going on with our situation. The reality was that God had led us to some things to help us on our healing journey, but those were not the things that brought healing; God did, and He always does. We found ourselves glorifying things and people who didn't deserve it. This was done unintentionally, but we had to realize we were not giving God all the glory He deserved. No one deserves it more than God. We had to humble ourselves enough to know that we could not simply do it on our own or figure it out. It had to be God's heavenly solution. We had tried to do it our way. It was like preparing a cart for a horse and then realizing that was not the cart God was going to use. We had to let that cart go and ask Him how He wanted to build it.

At times in our adoption journey, we felt we clearly heard God, so we stepped forward and took some risks. We were disappointed, but we knew we had heard God. We just couldn't shake it. This wasn't the first time we had been discouraged or gone through a loss. We had to choose how we were going to respond. When humans and free will are involved, things may change, but God will always bring good out of it. He can use anyone and anything. Even when something is God's will, it may not happen like we thought it would because other people made different decisions; God can still use all that.

The truth about your situation might be:

You had peace.

You heard from God clearly.

You obeyed what God said.

You loved and honored people well.

You gave God glory.

You still experienced disappointment and loss.

We had done this in our two adoption failures. We put ourselves out there, exercised our faith, and sacrificed. We had received promises from God that we knew would be fulfilled one day, but we didn't know when. Through this, God was developing our character because He knew we would need it to handle His dreams and promises!

It reminds me of the promises God gave Abram and Sarai (before their names were changed to Abraham and Sarah). Abram obeyed God and surrendered to His plan. God's will is perfect, and He never causes terrible or painful things to happen because it's not in His nature, but we have to realize we all have free will, which alters life's outcomes. God has given us all free will to make our own decisions and choices. We can involve God or not—it is our choice. Everyone gets to choose whether to align with God's will or not. He never causes these painful things to happen, like loss, failure, or family splits. However, He will use it to direct us back to the path He designed for us. He is such a loving Father, always redeeming and giving grace.

Of course, some situations are completely out of our control simply because we live in a fallen world. I want to honor that, as sometimes we experience things we didn't choose. Even in places in our lives where we experience negative things because of our choices, we can still give them to God, and He will bring beauty out of them if we let Him.

We often bring OUR plans to God and want Him to pick one of them to "sign off on." This is not the way God works. His thoughts are not our thoughts, and His ways are not our ways (Isa. 55:8). As we continue to lean in and become more like Him, our ways become His.

Radical Obedience (Melody) ✳——————————

I love the story of Jericho. I was reading about the radical obedience that Joshua and the Israelites had. God didn't ask for anyone's opinion on how to overtake Jericho, its king, and its people. God asked them for their obedience—unwavering obedience. God wanted them to march six days around the walls and then, on the seventh day, to blow their trumpets with a great shout. The Israelites and Joshua took that first crazy step of obedience and faith. In the natural, this sounded absolutely wild. Who would do that for six days and continue to wait for God to move? Most people would have to stop after one, two, or even three days. Each day, they kept taking radical steps of unwavering obedience. What if they had stopped? What if they had decided to do it their way? Think of all they would have missed. They would have cheated themselves out of victories from God. In the tension, God shows us where a measure of success is. It is being able to navigate outside of the promised land and in it. The Israelites had to experience this tension of the promise and the "not yet." They had to keep trusting God would come through for them.

I have to admit, it sure is hard to continue marching when we don't see God move the way we thought He would. It's difficult to trust what He is doing behind the scenes. We must shift our perspective to what God is doing instead of what He isn't doing. Choose to walk by faith and not by sight.

Take God at His word and hold fiercely to His promises! God will bring victory at the right time. God did exactly that for Joshua and the Israelites. Our victories never hinge on our ability or well-thought-out plans. They're dependent on unwavering obedience to God and trusting His plan. As spirit-filled believers who follow His voice, there is no limit to where God can lead us if we refuse to be hindered by our past. No matter the circumstances you were born into, God can bring you from the pasture to the palace!

In the story of Jericho, God received all the glory. Because of their obedience and surrendering of their plans, it became their highest form of worship for God. Authentic worship comes from surrender. You have to go through hard things to understand the weightiness of worship. Radical obedience requires us to follow the rules of God's world. Emotions and prayer will not substitute for radical obedience.

Our worship of God removes the obstacle to our victory, but we still have to go get our victory! Worship sets the stage to move in more authority in your situation. What the Israelites learned in the wilderness was no longer relevant to their new life in the promised land. The promised land represented grace. What you get by grace, sometimes you have to fight to keep in your life. The Israelites had to war for a land they did not build, but they had to obey God and watch how He would do it.

The interesting thing about the battle of Jericho is that they had the ark of the covenant with them. The ark of the covenant powerfully symbolized faith and God's presence. The tablets of the Mosaic law, a pot of manna, and Aaron's rod were found inside the ark. These represented God's presence, provision, and approval. They were reminders of what God had brought them through. Previously, the ark of the Lord had been a crucial object in helping the Israelites pass over the Jordan River into the promised land.

We must exercise surrender and obedience in the tension of a promise's fulfillment. In order to lay down how we want the end result to look, we must let go. It's not forgetting but letting go. You can let go of a loss in your life but not forget it. It will always be a part of you, but it needs to be an offering of surrender. God requires us to lay down what we are going through to give us the strength we need. In our weakness, He is strong.

When we faced not one but two failed adoptions, we remembered how God had brought us through before, and that gave us strength for the days ahead. The tension was building, and at times, it was uncomfortable, but we knew God would launch us into our breakthrough in His timing.

Tension before a breakthrough reminds me of a slingshot. When you put enough tension on the slingshot, it can catapult whatever you have farther away than without it. Your tension will eventually push destiny to fulfillment in God's timing. There is always a giant standing at the gateway of your destiny. Obedience and surrender knock down the enemies. What are the walls of Jericho before you? Where do you need to exercise surrender and obedience in your life? For some things, God will perform for you; for others, your strategic participation is critical to fulfilling the promise.

Today, keep taking step after step of obedience. Do not give up. Keep pursuing, keep declaring, keep trusting, and keep hoping! Don't stop short of your victory with God. I know you feel tired and weary, but keep going. God will be your strength. Because guess what? Generations depend on your ability to obey and surrender. It's crucial for those yet to be born.

Reflection:
~ Have you fully surrendered your situation to God?
~ How can you start walking in obedience to the Lord?

Prayer:
Lord, remind me of the promises You have spoken over my life. Help me contend for them and understand Your character and faithfulness in the tension. In Jesus's name, I pray. Amen.

IT'S TIME TO HAVE FAITH AND HOPE AGAIN

(HEALING INFERTILITY)

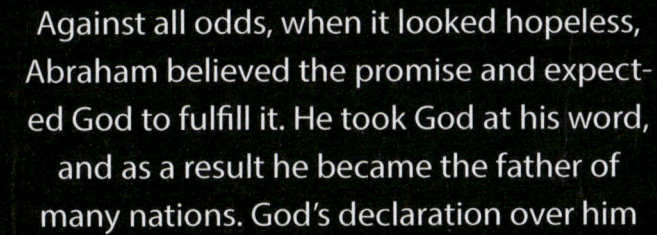

> Against all odds, when it looked hopeless, Abraham believed the promise and expected God to fulfill it. He took God at his word, and as a result he became the father of many nations. God's declaration over him came to pass: "Your descendants will be so many that they will be impossible to count!"
>
> *— Romans 4:18 TPT*

Imagine being in Abram and Sarai's shoes for a moment. You receive a promise from God, but it's been many years, and still hasn't happened. Do you lose hope? Do you question God's promise or if you heard God? Do you take matters into your own hands? Abram and Sarai probably had all those thoughts. In fact, they did take matters into their own hands as years went by since God wasn't making things happen in their timeline. Because of this, God let Ishmael be born, yet He still said the promised child was coming. Can you imagine the agony and even shame Sarai felt for not being able to carry her own child and give birth? In that culture, it was shameful. As both Abram and Sarai grew older, their hope probably got deferred at times. Our hope was deferred at times in our story. Hope deferred makes the heart sick, but hope is not a circumstance. It's a person—Jesus. What makes your heart sick when hope is deferred? The thing you hoped for, in this case, losing and waiting for children, is what made our hearts sick. Whenever we stop hoping, we stop believing and trusting!

Waiting for Fulfillment (Melody) ✳

Have you lost hope? Have you been through a situation that seems complicated to believe what God is speaking about your life? Abram is the perfect example of a hopeless situation that turned hope-filled. Fast-forward, and God would rip off the curtains of shame when Sarai became pregnant with Isaac. Yet even after the promised child, Abram (then called Abraham) was tested again when God asked him to give Isaac as a sacrifice. Can you imagine giving away the very thing you had longed for and prayed for so long?

How do you hold on to God's promises and words lightly, yet keep the faith for them? How do you contend for hope in the midst of opportunities for doubt? There are so many questions, but hang on tight as we closely examine Abram and Sarai's story.

Romans 4:18 says, "Against all hope, Abraham in hope believed and so became the father of many nations, just as it had been said to him, 'So shall your offspring be.'" I love Matthew Henry's commentary to help us understand the kind of hope Abram had:

✳ There was a hope against him, a natural hope. All the arguments of sense, and reason, and experience, which in such cases usually beget and support hope, were against him; no second causes smiled upon him, nor in the least favoured his hope. But, against all those inducements to the contrary, he believed; for he had a hope for him: He believed in hope, which arose, as his faith did, from the consideration of God's all-sufficiency. That he might become the father of many nations. Therefore God, by his almighty grace, enabled him thus to believe against hope, that he might pass for a pattern of great and strong faith to all generations. It was fit that he who was to be the father of the faithful should have something more than ordinary in his faith—that in him faith should be set in its highest elevation, and so the endeavours of all succeeding believers be directed, raised, and quickened. Or this is mentioned as the matter of the promise that he believed; and he refers to Gen. 15:5; So shall thy seed be, as the stars of heaven, so innumerable, so illustrious. This was that which he believed, when it was counted to him for righteousness, v. 6. And it is observable that this particular instance of his faith was against hope, against the surmises and suggestions of his unbelief. He had just before been concluding hardly that he should go childless, that one born in his house was his heir (v. 2, 3); and this unbelief was a foil to his faith, and bespeaks it a believing against hope.[25]

Abram carried a hope that expected good things were going to happen. That God's word was going to come to pass. When Isaac was finally born, it was just the beginning of God's promise. Abram's descendants would be numerous. Later, he had to continually trust God and listen to

25

Chapter Ten

Matthew Henry, *Matthew Henry's Commentary on the Whole Bible: Complete and Unabridged in One Volume* (Peabody: Hendrickson, 1994), 2203.

what God was currently saying; otherwise, Isaac would not have lived. Always contend for the breakthrough, but stay reliant on God's voice, not your ability. Learn to have enduring hope. In certain situations, what we say and do is critical to the measure of breakthrough we will experience. If you do not declare what God is saying with your mouth over your life, even though the Holy Spirit is moving and doors are open, it will be a limited realm of breakthrough. So many people cancel their yes to God by what they say. They say yes to the will of God, but then they find themselves saying they cannot accomplish it.

In Genesis 15, God made a promise and covenant with Abram. God told Abram that he would have a son and that his lineage would be as vast as the stars in the sky: "He took him outside and said, 'Look up at the sky and count the stars—if indeed you can count them.' Then he said to him, 'So shall your offspring be'" (Gen. 15:5).

Abram trusted every word God said. With a prophetic promise that still needed to be fulfilled, he had to contend with his doubts and timeline. He had to wait on God with faith and patience. God is faithful and will not disappoint us. When you get prophetic words and promises that have not come to pass yet, put your faith into action and declare out loud the word that is going to happen.

In Genesis 16, Abram had a son through Ishmael, but he was not the one God had chosen for the promise. That was still yet to be fulfilled. God would bless Ishmael, too, but not in the same way. As Abram and Sarai contended for God's word, there were thirteen years between chapters 16 and 17 that Sarai did not conceive. Talk about a long time to hold onto a promise as you grow older and older. Here's a revelation I learned as I read this story and looked at my circumstances. In the waiting, we can have a revelation of God's goodness. It increases our hope because we know He is good and faithful. This brings a new challenge—walking blameless before God. When we live in God's ways, we live in holiness. Abram inherited the kingdom while waiting because he walked blameless before God! God changed Abram's name to Abraham in chapter 17 (before Isaac was born) and declared that he had a new identity! A father of nations! Abram means an exalted father, but Abraham means a father of a multitude.

God literally changed the course of Abraham's life. A generational transfer would take place through Isaac. He not only changed Abraham's name but also Sarai's to Sarah—from a princess to a queen and from infertility to fertility. God gave them new names and a new destiny that would be fulfilled. God always sticks with His plan A. He doesn't have a plan B! Hope, in its very nature, encompasses faith, and hope is the soil in which faith puts its roots. Abraham activated his faith in what God said He was going to do. You, too, can activate your hope because you cannot have faith without hope.

Again, in Genesis 18, the promise and prophetic words are repeatedly spoken and emphasized. It was now getting close to fulfillment, but God knew Abraham and Sarah needed that encouragement to keep being faithful in the waiting. Before Isaac was born, Abraham prayed for Abimelech and his wife and servants to be healed from infertility, and they were. It was the first healing recorded in the Bible, prayed by Abraham. He prayed for the very thing he had not yet received! Faith sees the unseen. Faith is the confidence and character of Christ, and Abraham walked in this way.

Mind and Body Connection (Melody)

I have to be honest and say that we did not always have hope in every moment of our journey. As we mentioned in a previous chapter, there were many times we had doubt and disappointment. Having a healthy baby develop to full term is nothing short of a miracle. We had to choose to have hope and faith in God's promises for our lives without deciding what it would look like. Our fertility journey has been messy, painful, expensive, frustrating, disappointing, and draining. At the same time, it has been unique to us; it has made us lean into God, made us compassionate, tested our faith, and increased our longing to see Heaven on earth.

We didn't want to be just a statistic. According to the World Health Organization, one in six people globally is affected by infertility.[26] More than two million babies are stillborn each year.[27] One in four pregnancies ends in miscarriage.[28] We were a part of these statistics, and we didn't want to have that label anymore.

We are mind, body, and spirit. The physical part is a specific piece that is connected in a unique way. You know the feeling when you hear a bad report and get a knot in your stomach. You recognize the thoughts of stress that affect your back and neck pain. You know the feeling of being hopeless and letting your body suffer from a lack of self-care. I realized a few years into our journey of having children that my body would respond to thoughts I was having, emotions I was feeling, or when God was speaking to me. When God gave me a revelation or spoke to me, I usually felt peace, relaxation, or strength in my body. When I received negative reports from tests about what was going on in my body, I felt stress, aches and pains, and had poor sleep. When I wanted things to happen on my timeline, I got stressed and overwhelmed when it wasn't happening. When I saw or heard of drama in family or friend circles, my body would immediately feel the stress of it. At one point, it became so severe I couldn't be around specific people because I didn't know how to deal with how my body was responding negatively to it. It was making me physically sick. Now, I'm not blaming anyone because it was my choice to listen, believe, or let those things bother me rather than taking and giving them to God. After all, they

[26] World Health Organization: WHO, "1 in 6 people globally affected by infertility: WHO," *World Health Organization*, April 4, 2023,
https://www.who.int/news/item/04-04-2023-1-in-6-people-globally-affected-by-infertility/.
[27] World Health Organization: WHO, "Stillbirth," December 10, 2019,
https://www.who.int/health-topics/stillbirth#tab=tab_1.
[28] "The Unacceptable Stigma and Shame Women Face After Baby Loss Must End," World Health Organization, accessed March 23, 2025,
https://www.who.int/news-room/spotlight/why-we-need-to-talk-about-losing-a-baby/unacceptable-stigma-and-shame.

were not mine to carry.

Wanting to have a child is a deep desire. When it's not happening, and the world around you isn't healthy, it's easy to get anxious. Infertility affects many aspects of people's lives, and it certainly did for us. It affected my daily involvement in conversations, social activities, appointments, passions and hobbies, business and dreams, marriage and family, church community, and simple daily tasks and thoughts. It took over my thought life. Unknowingly, I identified with infertility instead of fertility, which God called us all to at the beginning of the Bible (Gen. 1:28). We are to speak over our future as God does. I wasn't doing that, and I needed a change, a different view, and a heavenly perspective. The battle of the mind and body are so intricately connected, and what we speak gives life or death. I couldn't sit back and watch my hopes and dreams die.

After two miscarriages, I started taking my health more seriously and pursued deeper testing. After a couple of years, I had done a lot of detoxing, changing my lifestyle, eating habits, and sleep. I still was not where I needed to be, but I was much better than where I started. I had suffered from extremely low energy and fatigue, not sleeping well, acne, excruciating periods, PMS, brain fog, mold toxicity, parasites, heavy metals, and more. I won't bore you with every detail, but for eight years, I saw twelve different people from the holistic and medical worlds combined. It was a lot of telling my story over and over and adding more information each time. I tried so many different tests and therapies, you name it, except IUI or IVF. We never went that direction because I was able to get pregnant, but it was more about being able to carry a healthy baby to term, my egg quality, our DNA, etc. Insurance would not cover any of the costs of IUI or IVF, and so it would be like buying a new car in cost—all the therapies, supplements, and testing we did medically and holistically cost well over $100,000. Our insurance covered very little, but we had made the choice that we were going to dig deeper and be as healthy as we could be. What did we have if we didn't have good health to live the life God called us to?

Faith in the Wrong Things (Melody) ✳━━━━━━━━━━

Year after year went by, and we got into many roadblocks and ditches—so many opinions of doctors, health coaches, naturopaths, etc. It was hard for me to navigate what was right for me. I would see some progress but not complete healing. I kept searching and asking God to show us our next steps. After Kanaan's stillbirth and going into adoption, we figured we would lay down all our options and pursue what we felt God was leading us to. In His kindness, He would steer us as we took a step. An important lesson we learned along the way was giving God the glory. No doctor, health guru, herb, supplement, medication, procedure, or therapy could receive all the glory. Only God is worthy of all the glory. Because we were not seeing progress, we would find someone else we felt was willing to listen to our story and help in a different way. We wanted things to happen on our timeline, but they didn't. God was working behind the scenes even though we needed to be reminded in each step. In the spiritual realm, the reality is that there are no timelines!

Time and time again, we found ourselves giving glory to different ways of thought, protocols, or whatever seemed revolutionary at the time. We didn't do this intentionally, but we were so desperate for answers that sometimes, we believed we had figured it out. What we found wrong was not just one thing but many. God would have to bring healing in ways other people and the world could not.

When I was researching adoption, I came across a woman selling herbal fertility kits from another country. I followed her account, and she had many testimonies from clients who had used her products with excellent results. Suddenly, false hope filled me with the thought that "maybe this would be the thing that works." It seemed too good to be true, but I couldn't get over what women said they were experiencing and the healthy babies they had.

At that time, I had already used a lot of good quality herbs through my herbalist training, and continue to this day, but there were some unique herbs I had never heard of that were unavailable in the United States. This grabbed my attention. I talked on the phone with this person and messaged back and forth, asking many questions. After days and many conversations, I decided to purchase the kit. To make a long story short, I took a risk out of desperation to buy the herbs only to be let down that, in the end, it was a complete scam. We lost a couple thousand dollars and had nothing to show for it except the feeling of being taken advantage of, which turned to frustration. Looking back, I'm shocked that we fell for it (our personalities are very cautious), but because of desperation, the enemy led us down another path that seemed promising. However, it was a counterfeit of what God wanted to do in our lives. It was another way the enemy tried to get us to strive for our healing. You see, anytime God has brought life or a promise, Satan tries to steal, kill, destroy, or provide a counterfeit. Desperation for the wrong thing can bring emptiness.

Through God's kindness and conviction, we learned that we cannot attribute our healing to our efforts. We had to depend on Him and thank Him for each day of healing and progress He provided. There is no limit to where God can lead us if we refuse to be hindered by our past circumstances. Our focus needed to be shifted from a medical or wellness cure and protocol to a God who still heals today in whatever capacity and way He wants! He was going to get the glory in the end. Faith denies a negative place of influence, but it does not deny a problem existing. I am not saying to deny what you are going through or experiencing. It's real, and it's painful. What I am saying is do not allow your experience to influence you in a way that causes you to lose faith in God and how He wants to heal. If we had all the answers, then what good is faith?

Of course, God uses both medical and holistic wellness communities. Sometimes, healing comes from surgery, or sometimes, it comes instantly (like in the case of a miracle). Healing is a process, whereas miracles are supernaturally instant. It all dawned on me one day. You can have a healthy life by stewardship, but you can only have a healed life by faith. I wanted a miracle to happen, but I also knew that God could heal me in the process. I needed to have expectations of both and wait on God.

God Gets the Last Word (Melody) ✳━━━━━━━━━━━━━

Our faith did not come from striving; it came from surrender. We did things we knew were good for our bodies, like eating well, biohacking, using natural herbs and plants God created, and much more. We waited actively for God to move. We would take a step, and then He would have to adjust our steps if we wanted to go in a different direction from His plan. That is a good place to be: dependent and expectant on God.

I had heard of miracles and healing of people from fertility issues, and I knew that God wanted me to be whole because He came to the world to not only save us but also break the curse of sin in the world. God created us to be able to reproduce, but sin in the world has brought pain and heartache in this area where some of us experience loss or infertility. The reality with God is that there is no infertility in Heaven, so we should pray and declare that Heaven's will and realities be brought to earth in God's timing. It is His will for us to be healed and made whole. It is His will for us to be able to have a child or children (in whatever way that comes, biological or not). God's timing may not come early in your healing, but He is never late! As we waited and did what we knew to do with our human limitations, God developed fruit in us that would honor Him. Our faith was multiplied.

This waiting led me to a book called God's Plan for Pregnancy by Nerida Walker. I highly recommend it if you want to dive deep into Scripture on everything, including conception, pregnancy, loss, etc. It changed how I thought about what we were going through and how Jesus had broken the curse of barrenness, childbirth pain, and infertility. Essentially, it addresses the curse of women. You see, barrenness came with the fall. The blessing of bearing fruit was corrupted. Barrenness is listed as a curse in Deuteronomy 28:18: "The fruit of your womb will be cursed, and the crops of your land,

and the calves of your herds and the lambs of your flocks."

God created all things to be good and fruitful. He never intended for anyone to be cursed. After the fall of Adam and Eve, the sin dweller Satan took charge to corrupt man's nature and God's plan. In Nerida's book, she writes, "Provision was corrupted into lack. Prosperity and wealth was corrupted into debt and poverty. Health was corrupted into sickness and disease. Fruitfulness was corrupted into barrenness."[29]

Even though sin entered the world, God had a redemptive plan. Jesus paid the price for all sin in full. He redeemed each one of us from the curse! Can you and do you believe that? Infertility, miscarriage, and loss are all different forms of sickness, but His healing and fullness are available today. This also means that although we may face complications in our fertility journeys, we do not have to accept setbacks as the end of the story. We have the power in Jesus's name to take authority over the issues we encounter. Galatians 3:13 says Jesus "redeemed us from the curse of the law!" God also said in Galatians 3:7, 9, and 29 that those who have faith in Christ would be blessed through Abraham's seed.

In Abraham's story, even his son and daughter-in-law suffered from infertility, but God brought healing. The enemy always tries to discourage us, make us dwell on bad reports or circumstances, believe lies, and bring death. We must choose to believe what God says and walk in His truth. Because we live in a fallen world, there is still pain and loss, but it's not what God wants. He wants everyone who wants it to experience life and fruitfulness. It's His will. The enemy fights so hard to bring chaos into our fertility journeys because he knows what God's promises are to us.

You might be thinking about the diagnoses you got, the loss you endured, or the physical condition your body or partner's body is in. You might have just received a test result (like we did while writing this chapter) that was discouraging. You might think having children is impossible

[29] Nerida Walker, *God's Plan for Pregnancy: From Conception to Childbirth and Beyond* (Harrison House Publishing: Tulsa, 2004), 150.

because of everything you have already "tried."

God wants us to bring these things into submission to Him. Nothing is too big or too small for Him. Part of our inheritance in Christ is healing. Bring your conditions in submission to God's truth and declare Scripture over them.

A personal step for me was not claiming a diagnosis in my body. After Kanaan passed, I had an ultrasound done and some blood tests to make sure there were no infections from having a stillbirth. The clinic I went to diagnosed me with PCOS. I had a decision to make. Would I come under that diagnosis or surrender it to God and not receive it?

I realized there was significance in the words I spoke over myself, especially when I was with other people. I came to understand that saying, "I have" PCOS or (whatever your diagnosis is) was reinforcing it. I had to start changing the way I talked about it. Instead of saying, "I have," I would say, "Doctors diagnosed me with (fill in the blank)," or "I have been dealing with symptoms of (fill in the blank)." It wasn't denying what tests showed or what the doctors said, but I was not going to come under the authority of the label put on me.

I have a background in holistic health, but when a diagnosis came to me personally, it felt different. What could I do naturally to negate these symptoms and root issues while being careful not to receive the diagnosis? Much of it was about the words that came out of my mouth and my thoughts about my future. Even now, sometimes, I catch myself becoming a victim. If you have been diagnosed with something or have been told something negative about your body, you do not have to receive it. Don't let your problem be more significant than your God is!

Every day, give it to God. We are not meant to carry these heavy burdens or a diagnosis. Again, it's not denying it but changing our focus to put it on God as our healer. God never meant for you to have that diagnosis or health issue. He is always willing to heal. The diagnosis others have given us needs to come under submission to Christ. Renew your mind until you believe in your heart that God wants to bring restoration to your body. Of course, we do not know the timing, but we can't give up hope. It could be any moment, any day! God's resurrection power of life can overcome your adverse natural circumstances.

The Bible proclaims God's victory in fertility. The stories of Abraham and Sarah, Isaac and Rebekah, Jacob and Rachel, Zechariah and Elizabeth, and many more reveal how God intervened in their situations. David and I had to get to the spot where we truly trusted God and His finished work at the cross. Giving up our control in every aspect and not putting faith in our efforts was crucial. Even in writing this now, I strive (in a good way) to enter a place of rest with God and trust in His provision of healing however He wants to do it. I had previously put hope in doctors, protocols, therapies, and the like, but I now wanted to put all my hope in God, putting all my eggs in His basket! No plan B, but God's plan A.

Because of God's new covenant, we are seated in heavenly places with Him. He is waiting for us to agree with His word! It's not that I deny what may be going on in my body or what tests show, but it's about agreeing with the better word that God speaks. It's declaring the realities of Heaven into your body here and now on earth. God wants us to be well and fertile even now. It's part of His original design! If you keep your focus on the natural realm and not God's reality, it's easy to get discouraged. We've been there.

Guard what you allow in and out. Maybe you are dealing with severe complications and have heard the words, "I'm sorry, but you will probably never conceive or have a child." Do not let that be the last word! Let God's truth be the last word. He has done miracles for people with such complicated situations that the world cannot deny His power. The Holy Spirit has the answers and solutions to what is going on in our bodies. We just need to tap in. Don't you think it's time to have hope in God for your situation? Maybe it's hard to believe that God can do it. Maybe there is fear to take the next step. It's okay to feel that, but do not stay in that state of mind. Fear can keep you from the best that God has for you. It's not too late to reach out to God and ask Him to renew your mind with His truth and belief for healing.

✷　Take a moment right now to pray this prayer:

God, I repent of coming into agreement with any lies that the enemy or others have spoken over me, my spouse, and my body. I ask for Your forgiveness and to be restored to Your heart's desire for wholeness in my life. Please help me know Your truth when a diagnosis, fear, or test result comes back. Help me to trust You and Your words that never change. I ask for healing for _____ (be specific here). I believe You can bring healing and fertility to my body/our bodies. Thank You, Jesus, in advance for Your restoration. I pray in Jesus's name. Amen!

Stewards of Healing (David) ✷━━━━━━━━━━━━━━━━

If you or anyone close to you has been struggling or is struggling with infertility or recurrent pregnancy loss, I don't have to tell you how hard it is to find answers. At the end of the day, I believe there are just a lot of things we, as humans, don't understand and don't know about the human body. God is God, and we are not! That being said, technology, medicine, research, biohacking, natural health, and wellness gurus have come a long way in understanding disease, its causes, and how to heal physical properties. Before we dive in just a bit, it's essential to understand some things. The first is that, as we've already covered, humans are complicated, intricate, unique, multifaceted beings. We have a spirit, a soul, and a body. Even though we try to compartmentalize one over the other in our Western way of thinking, I think this is arrogance and foolishness. Real (sozo) healing requires focusing on all of it.

The second thing to understand is this: We are not doctors, and this is not medical advice. Most of this book is about healing spiritually, mentally, emotionally, and relationally. However, we'd be holding back too much if we didn't dive in (if only for a chapter) to some of the things we've found helpful in our healing journey.

We haven't arrived, and we won't arrive until we get to Heaven, but we have seen measures of breakthrough and found methods and schools of thought that have brought us to levels of physical health that we would have never thought possible ten years ago. At the point of writing this chapter, we've tried everything short of IUI/IVF—and we are even open to that if necessary as we've leaned into the process of surrender and obedience to God.

We never stop! We continue to dig, pray, trust, believe, declare, work hard, and then dig some more while ensuring we are not striving alone. As I write this, we're going in for more advanced testing this week, and it's been almost a decade of this! Sometimes, we feel like human Petri dishes, but we pray and trust that our pain and process have become our purpose.

We believe that God wastes nothing, and we aim to be good stewards of the research and resources we've come across. We believe that God expects us to steward our bodies well with the things He has created, as Scripture says: "Do you not know that your bodies are temples of the Holy Spirit, who is in you, whom you have received from God? You are not your own; you were bought at a price. Therefore honor God with your bodies" (1 Cor. 6:19–20). So, at the risk of vastly understating these things, we'll offer some conclusions and resources at the back of the book in a section titled "Fertility, Loss, and Miscarriage Support" to help you get started with lots of practical steps!

We changed our whole lifestyle because we finally found something that made sense to us in the natural realm. If we got healthier as God intended our bodies to be, we would reproduce as God also created healthy bodies to do. Infertility is not in Heaven, and loss is not in Heaven. Therefore, if we are to co-labor with God to bring Heaven to earth, it's our yearning that we don't see infertility and loss here either. We have an uphill battle, but with

God, anything is possible.

From the Experts (David) ✳━━━━━━━━━━━━━━━━━

We met so many dear friends along the way. One person who still makes a profound impact on our spiritual, physical, and relational health is Dr. Suzy. She is a mighty warrior in the kingdom of God. She's networked with some giants in the health and wellness world and is so kind to share those resources with us and many others. I met Dr. Suzy way back when I was playing baseball in college. The repetitive motion of practicing my swing, along with heavy days of lifting, was putting quite a stress on my spine and body in general, so much so that I ended up developing a stress fracture in my lower back that ended my athletic career at the time.

I couldn't find anything that helped, including traditional chiropractic adjustments. At the time, I thought she was a genius and could read my body and condition in ways others couldn't. I now realize that she has a close relationship with the Holy Spirit, and He helped her help me. I remember her explaining to me that I just had chronic inflammation that started in my gut, and she thought that if we addressed that, it'd help my back pain. I thought it was crazy, but I was desperate, so I did a three-day cleanse with a cultured whey probiotic drink and cleaned up my diet. She adjusted me through my stomach, which was unusual and uncomfortable, but my back was pain-free in just a few weeks! I've never had issues since, and it's been about fifteen years. I can swing a baseball bat, play golf, archery hunt, and do many things today completely pain-free!

Dr. Suzy is our dear friend, and she's been a vital cog in our journey. She helped us reconcile the medical and natural worlds and taught us that they both have strengths and weaknesses. She is a person who has so much going on, but she is always a text or call away. I just can't say enough about the wisdom she's shared and how she's guided us to eat and live the way God intended us to. One of the most incredible ways she's helped us is by leveraging some of her friendships and connections. I still pinch myself to this day, but early on in our marriage, she introduced us to another person I feel honored to know: Jordan Rubin.

Jordan is a legend and giant in the health and wellness space. He is a New York Times best-selling author and co-founder (with Dr. Josh Axe) of Ancient Nutrition, a unique and reputable supplement company. He is probably most well-known for the multiple renditions of his book, The Maker's Diet. If you want to start somewhere in your health journey, start there. That book is timeless, and the wisdom is profound. If you read and follow that, you will be well on your way to a vastly changed spiritual and physical life. I love how he parallels biblical principles with how we can be the most physically healthy.

I admire Jordan because he takes no shortcuts. The call on his life is palpable. It would be easy for him to sit back on his haunches and live off his success. However, he has taken the hard road and the road that God has called him to. In his kindness, he let Melody and I visit with him, babysit his kids during an event, and tour his regenerative, beyond-organic farms and ranches in Missouri and Tennessee!

He and his team are truly changing how we farm and eat for the better. It was incredible to see an ancient breed of zebu cattle that produced milk with A2/A2 protein similar to goats' or sheep's milk. Everything is genuinely grass-fed and grass-finished. The products are even better than organic standards. Everything works together in a symbiotic relationship. The pastures, chickens, ducks, cattle, goats, water buffalo, woods, and greenhouses are the healthiest I've seen. They are rebuilding the soil by growing food without tilling. It's a truly regenerative experience, and his farms are creating some of the healthiest foods and supplements you can buy. Many supplement companies are just private-labeling something that many other people sell. Ancient Nutrition is different. I saw with my own eyes where he grows herbs that they use in their products. They are organic, regenerative, and grown in the heartland of America.

At the risk of sounding like a commercial, I realized with his help that our food industry is corrupt and unhealthy. They've been spraying things and altering things in a way that has caused or contributed to many of our chronic diseases today! They say GMO stands for "genetically modified organism." I think it stands for, "God, move over!" Big pharma and big food have come up with systems to keep us sick but not dead. GMOs, Roundup, pesticides, drugs, vaccines, and the like all contribute to a society that is dependent on the system. Jordan and his team have taught us and many people how to homestead sustainably and live healthier, simpler, more fulfilling lives.

So, with the help of some amazing friends, practitioners, and mentors, Melody and I changed everything in our lifestyle. We cut out food that was inflammatory to us and did intense detox regimens that included sauna, red light, castor oil, coffee enemas, acupuncture, Mercier therapy, and even advanced blood ozone techniques to get rid of mold and viral infections. We ate and still try to eat organic and whole food diets built on grass-fed and finished protein, along with fats like A2/A2 butter, ghee, or coconut oil. If that sounds like too much, it doesn't have to be expensive or complicated. Start with simple organic proteins and veggies. It's costly when you try to replace the junk with "healthier" junk! Avoid processed foods and start with the Maker's diet. Dig deeper with the right practitioner or doctor with testing if you are still not getting results.

We (and you) can find the reasons for disease and take the necessary steps to fix them with the Holy Spirit, the right time, expertise, and resources. At the same time, that journey can become an idol in and of itself, so through it all, we have to stay connected to the vine (John 15). Stay humble. Realize that God leads you to and through all of it. Be obedient. He may ask you to step out and do some things that seem crazy, but He will use all of it to make us more like Him!

You might sometimes get it wrong and start to worship the healing modality over the healer (even subconsciously). As we've learned, there is a fine line. God gets it. He wants you healed more than you do. Just repent and repent again. In His kindness, He uses all of it as you consecrate it to Him. Realize that your story is unique, and your journey and route will be too. The sooner you can surrender the way you want it to look in exchange for the journey He's taking you on, the sooner you'll find peace in the journey. There are so many rabbit holes that you can go down, and I encourage you to do so if you feel His peace in them.

A Yielded Life (Melody) ✴

Our fertility wasn't just about what was going on physically, as we have already mentioned. It was mind, body, and spirit. We had to step back and discover how God changed us while waiting. It was not about what we wanted but, ultimately, what God wanted. I don't know what God will do in your life. I don't know how a child or children will come to you in your life. It might be biological, through adoption, or through the influence of being a spiritual parent to a child who doesn't have that in his or her life. No matter how it comes, God knows your desires; He gave them to you. It's okay to ask God for a child! It just needs to come from a spot where we would rather become more like Him than idolize what we want.

I remember a counseling session David and I had after losing Kanaan. The counselor asked us, "What if you never have another child? Will you let God be enough for you?" I felt a deep gulp in my throat. He was right. We couldn't idolize having a child more than our great God. Our weighty and deep desire to have children sometimes led us to wonder what life was worth if we did not get to experience being parents. The truth is that our life matters because of God—each breath, each day. I had to change my idolizing of children to idolizing God our Creator. He knew my deep desires, and I could continue to bring and lay them down before Him, emotions and all. We had to have hands open to receive so that God could take what we had and give us something better while becoming more like Him.

Hebrews 6:15 says, "And so after waiting patiently, Abraham received what was promised." Abraham's descendants were the fulfillment of God's spoken word. In the waiting, Abraham inherited the kingdom. God had counted him as righteous. Keep in mind that Abraham never saw the rest of his descendants besides Isaac, but he knew God would fulfill His word through generations. God often gives us these promises, and we must learn to be faithful with the small progress and waiting. In that time of waiting and praying big prayers (not by our own strength), we inherit the kingdom. It's not about receiving what God has promised exactly the way we expect or hope; it's about becoming more like Him. Abraham was known for his faith and didn't even wait perfectly, but his waiting brought an inheritance of the kingdom for his future descendants. Our decisions today make a way for future generations to inherit the kingdom.

God uses our yielded lives. We can trust Him as we become more like Him. When wanting to be faithful and wait well, we sometimes forget that we need Him to invade our lives! No matter the test results, we knew God could take care of it. Posturing our lives in a way where Heaven can invade was risky, scary, and messy, but God loved us and cared about all the details. God waits on us and speaks prophetic words so we can have a life where Heaven can invade.

Before we ever had any losses with our children, we received a prophetic word from God a year after we were married. It spoke about our future and gave us wisdom that we would need to hold fast to God in our marriage and family. Prophetic words are conceived within before they are birthed externally. God knew we would come into multiple birthing seasons, physically and metaphorically. We needed this seed to steward, plant in our hearts, and water consistently. Later on, we would see the fruit. In Abraham's case, it would be generations after him. The tension between the promise and its fulfillment, as we talked about in the previous chapter, is the gap in between, which is faith.

Faith upon a declaration is what makes things come to pass, not declarations alone. Unless the Lord is upon it, there is no real momentum. We prayed, fasted, read Scripture, wrote out declarations, you name it. These were all good things, but God was watching to see how we would steward His words. We had to be careful not to make the prophetic words an idol. Our focus needed to be on God, the giver of life-filled words. Stewarding His words is knowing what His nature is like and knowing we can't do it without Him.

Again, this is where Heaven can invade, and breakthroughs happen. God can use any amount of faith! Let go of where you are and step into the gap of faith. In the gap is where we have no ability, but God does. When we get a word for our life, we often think it will be easy to step into. It simply is not! Many times, we are not equipped for it. The Lord calls you into spaces and circumstances you are not fully equipped for. Dependence on Him will cause us to do what we never could have dreamed or imagined doing.

You could be one step away from your breakthrough. Step into the gap today. Strengthen your faith. Feed on His Word (Scripture), His character, and His goodness. If we look at Genesis 22, we see Abraham's faith is tested again, but this time in a big way: giving up his own son. A new revelation will always bring a new test. Abraham probably didn't know God was testing him, but he passed the test of faith. God asked him to sacrifice his son Isaac, who, at the time, was likely in his teenage years or even possibly a young adult. God knew Abraham's love for Isaac, so it indeed would be a sacrifice for him to offer to God.

True worship always involves a sacrifice. Abraham knew that God's promise involved Isaac and the future generations that would come from him. He had such great faith that God would provide a sacrifice, or maybe he even thought God would resurrect Isaac. When we are faithless, He remains faithful. As the story goes, the Lord provided a ram for the offering instead of Isaac. Abraham passed God's test of faith! Because of it, the Lord declared that his seed would bless the entire world! Wow. His faith yielded to God even when it didn't make sense. Faith will carry us through the most severe trials as we obey the Holy Spirit before fully understanding. Step into faith, and be brave. Your healing is in Jesus. Resolve in your heart to choose faith over fear in your circumstance!

Reflection:
~ How can you increase your faith and hope in God for your situation?
~ How can you partner with the healing that Christ already paid for on the cross?

Prayer:
Lord, right now, I need hope. Increase my faith and hope today. Help me to see what You are doing in the spiritual when I cannot see it in the natural. Thank You for being the only hope I need. I pray in Jesus's name. Amen.

Chapter 11
SUDDENLY, MIRACLES HAPPEN

Let us hold unswervingly to the hope we
profess, for he who promised is faithful.

— *Hebrews 10:23*

At this point in your journey, maybe your faith, hope, and trust have been strengthened, and you think to yourself, "Nothing is impossible for God." After our second failed adoption, we were disappointed but were choosing to trust that God could do anything. We sought God and asked Him if adoption was still the right thing to pursue. At the same time, we began working with a different naturopath, and she explained how she thought she could help us on our fertility journey. It was an investment we were willing to make as we waited on God. It felt painful, though, to think about stepping out and taking a risk again with adoption. We didn't know what would be on the other side of saying "yes" again.

Have a Little Faith (Melody)

As we considered our next steps, we were reminded of encouraging words and prayers with Scripture from a few specific friends who spoke over us as we waited to hear what the past birth mom's decision was going to be. In the spiritual realm, they had not given up! You need people willing to take risks and call Heaven to earth in your circumstances. Their faith can help lift you up when your faith may be weak, just like Aaron and Moses (Ex. 17)!

As we took a few weeks to pray and process together, we decided to get active again with all the other agencies except the one we got matched with previously. We told that agency that our hearts were not open to risky situations right now unless the baby was already born and both birth parents had already signed and chosen us. They told us our options would be greatly reduced, but they respected our decision.

It had only been three weeks since the last failed adoption. November came, and we were still waiting but becoming hopeful again. We got a call on November 10 (the day the previous baby was supposed to be born). I was driving home from town when our former adoption agent called me. I thought that was odd, but I decided to pick up. I thought for a moment that the other birth mom had changed her mind. Since David was not with me, we called her back half an hour later. Little did we know that call would change our lives forever.

She proceeded to tell us that a baby girl had been born on November 4, and the birth parents had both signed their rights over that morning. They had picked us, and the agency wanted to know if we wanted to move forward and say yes to this precious baby. We were in complete shock! Joy overtook us. The process of suddenly was finally happening. We could not believe it, but we had to. God was answering many prayers that had been prayed, and as He worked behind the scenes on our behalf, He was invading our story for His glory. I realized at that moment that the exact words I had communicated to the agency in previous weeks were the same words she called to tell us. Our words truly are powerful, and God hears us!

After that call, David and I hugged and prayed with gratitude and hope. We had a couple of days to make a forever decision. It would be official if we wanted to step into this gift that God was clearly giving us. Our baby girl was born at 29.3 weeks and was in the NICU. She was born weighing two pounds and eleven ounces and now was underweight. We knew this would entail a lot being in the NICU with her for potentially two months, and we had to get our finances together immediately. We could not fly to her until we paid the at-risk fee. We prayed and decided, without a doubt, that this risk was completely worth it. We did not know then what could potentially come from being born so early, but they told us she was healthy, and they didn't see any reason for her not to be. A huge smile came over our faces as we realized God was simultaneously redeeming our story and hers. We said yes, had a day to pack our bags, and flew to Florida. It was a whirlwind, for sure. I remember frantically running around the house, packing everything into suitcases as fast as I could. It was an adrenaline rush!

November 15, 2023, we walked up to the hospital front desk to get our guest passes. A kind man led us to the NICU and brought us to our baby girl. Once we stepped into the NICU, it quickly got intense. Our daughter was so tiny and hooked up to so many monitors while having oxygen pressure help her lungs. Tears overcame us as we saw her perfect tiny body. She was our golden nugget from God. We named her Havilah Faith because we had to "have a little faith" in this journey to her. Havilah also represented gold, reminding us of the land of Havilah in the Bible. We now would have two children named after biblical lands. God was giving us another "promised land."

They let us have time with her the entire day. The next few days, we signed placement papers, and we were officially her guardians. There would be a lot more to the finalizing of adoption, but for now, she needed to grow and develop before she could come home. In the following days and weeks, we were there every day. We didn't want to leave her sight! We would take shifts and trade-offs so she could have skin-to-skin with each of us and develop an attachment to us both.

Havilah ended up being in the NICU for six weeks before we could go home with her. After leaving the NICU, we had to wait for clearances to return to Minnesota. Being in the NICU is hard. If you have had any experience, you know the intricacies and tragedies that can exist there. I remember one evening, after just being there a few days, a baby boy passed away in the unit next to Havilah. It was so scary and immediately brought me back to Kanaan's birth. It was emotional and complex, but it was the reality that was there. Many days, I would watch David speak declarations over Havilah and sing, and we would pray for her development, protection, and health.

There were many things in this situation we couldn't change; we had to trust God even in those moments. I remember thinking, "If He got us here, He will get us to the other side safely with smiles of joy on our faces." There were so many sweet moments. She would smile often. I remember one nurse explaining how she was praying and telling Havilah that her parents were coming (us). We had given her lots of love and care there, and Christmas was coming soon. On December 19, we were discharged from the NICU. Oh, how nervous we were! This extremely fragile four-pound baby girl was a miracle, and life with her was just beginning. Days later, we were boarding a flight home and arrived just before Christmas—a Christmas miracle.

We were experiencing our "Isaac" moment. We waited on God, trusted, took risks, kept the faith, increased our hope, and surrendered. We had cried and pounded our fists into the floor, desperate for God to move. Now, here we were on the other side of the process, experiencing the suddenly. Suddenly, the heavens spilled open, and a miracle happened.

The Lexham Bible Dictionary defines the biblical word MIRACLE (dynamis) as "An event that defies common expectations of behavior and subsequently is attributed to a superhuman agent; an occurrence that demonstrates God's involvement in the course of human affairs."[30] You might be reading this book and our journey thinking, "Wow, that's a cool story, but I still haven't seen the 'suddenly' happen to my family." If God did it for Abraham, He can do it for you. He wants to be involved in our everyday experiences and struggles. In each story of barrenness recorded in the Bible, God miraculously brought a child. Sarah, Rebekah, Rachel, Hannah (Samuel's mother), Samson's mother, and Elizabeth (John the Baptist's mother) all experienced barrenness, yet God provided a miracle in each of their stories. Let's take a look at Rebekah and Isaac:

✳ Now these are the records of the descendants of Isaac, Abraham's son: Abraham was the father of Isaac. Isaac was forty years old when he married Rebekah, the daughter of Bethuel the Aramean (Syrian) of Paddan-aram, the sister of Laban the Aramean. Isaac prayed to the Lord for his wife, because she was unable to conceive children; and the Lord granted his prayer and Rebekah his wife conceived [twins]. (Gen. 25:19–21 AMP)

Isaac was Abraham's son, and his wife Rebekah dealt with infertility, but God provided another miracle. This time with twins! God would continue to provide for Abraham's line, his seed. Think about this. All of this happened in the Old Testament. When Jesus came and broke the curse of the law (Gal. 3:13), this also means He broke the curse of childbirth pain and being unable to have children. He became the curse in our place! We no longer have to live with the attitude of foreboding or believe that everything has to be painful. When we do that, we come under agreement with the enemy.

30

Chapter Eleven

Ronald D. Roberts, "Miracle," *The Lexham Bible Dictionary*, ed. John D. Barry et al. (Bellingham, WA: Lexham Press, 2016).

We have to come under agreement with God, the King of kings and Lord of lords. He is Jehovah Rapha, Hebrew for "the Lord who heals." We cannot deny that we have access to Him and what He can do. As believers, we must learn to live from a state of mind that realizes Jesus paid for our healing. Whether we have seen that come to fruition or not, He has already done it in the past, present, and future. The moment we received salvation, we were healed. Yes, it takes time for our human minds and bodies to catch up with what God has already said, but He will bring restoration at a specific time.

When you can live a life of surrender, asking God to bring healing in whatever way He wants, He will do it according to His and Heaven's timing. Don't be swayed by your timing. I don't have all the answers. Why do some people have children in this life and others do not? I do not know. It's part of the mystery. Sometimes, healing or miracles occur in seed form. The Greek word sperma means "seed" and is related to the seed and legacy, which brings a holy conception of miracles. The seed may start small and build. There are so many factors that we will never truly know until we are fully restored with Christ. However, I will never give up hope or belief for it.

As we write this, we still wait and believe in healthy biological children from our seed. Just like Abraham, we believe God is faithful and will continue to produce generations that will glorify Him, no matter how that looks. You may find yourself in a similar situation or know someone living a similar journey. God knows the agony you have experienced. He knows your heart and your desires. He also knows how your story will end with redemption. Everyone's story can end with redemption, whether on this earth or in the next. We do not know what it will look like, and we cannot promise; however, we know He is a God who still does miracles whenever He wants! Sometimes, it's just a prayer away, even if you have prayed hundreds of prayers. Sometimes, it's just a moment of surrender or taking a risk away. For our daughter, it was all of this and more.

We will never know until we take those steps and continue to get our hopes up. Don't let disappointment steal your hope for a miracle. Miracles are part of the mystery of God. He is always willing, yet He waits in His perfect timing in ways we sometimes cannot comprehend. I think He likes us to be in that spot—solely dependent on Him. Miracles rarely happen in a place that doesn't have cooperation with God. Meet with Him, and have Him be the center of your experience. The more time you spend with Him, the more you become calibrated when He does something. When you are faced with an impossible situation, it's the perfect opportunity to let Heaven invade! God has to show up. There is no other option. He lives in the natural and supernatural realms at the same time. We have a limited experience and mindset, and that's where we must learn to release how we think God will come through for us. Don't limit God. Sit at His table and eat of His Word and His promises. Believe God for the best.

God Still Moves (David) ✱━━━━━━━━━━━━━━━━━━

I often find myself wondering what moves the heart of God. I find myself in the tension between knowing what God can do and even what He wills to do, yet I do not see it or experience it in my present circumstances. I see so many Christians give up on the idea of miracles, healings, prophecy, and even prayer because they've tried it once or twice or even a hundred times and didn't see the results they wanted. People get hurt and disappointed, and honestly, I get it. I understand the temptation to go down the cessationist ditch, that these miracles and wonders were only for a specific time, and those times seem to have expired. It's human nature to get in those places because we want to control and understand things. There is nothing wrong with the desire to grow in knowledge; God wants us to be good stewards of our minds, revelations, and actions. However, Bill Johnson's quote is so profound in these moments: "The level of revelation God gives you will always be equal to the level of mystery you're willing to live with. And the inability to live with mystery is your resistance to childlikeness. It's childlikeness that gives us access to dimensions and realms of the kingdom that you can't get in any other way."[31]

It's okay to want more information. It's okay, and you are encouraged to dig deeper and deeper into Scripture, sermons, podcasts, books, and any other media you can think of to find the answers and the keys to these things. Why do some people get healed and others don't? Why do some prophetic words seem to come to pass while others don't? Why does God miraculously provide finances for one person but seemingly not for another? It's easy to write these things off as if God doesn't move in these ways anymore. It's equally as easy to fall into the ditch of trying to figure out the formula and crack God's code. Both of those things are cop-outs. They are the easy path of least resistance we humans like to take.

You see, I think it's clear as you look at Scripture and even modern history that God still does move in signs and wonders for people when they ask. It's also worth noting that God is creative. He doesn't do it the same way every time. He shows up in new and fresh ways, and if you get caught up in the religious structure of it all, you miss Him. So, what is the key to a breakthrough? What is the key to seeing miracles happen in your life, family, city, and nation? The common thread in every miracle, sign, wonder, healing, prophetic utterance, move of God, revival, and even salvation is hope. At some point along the way, a child of God gets their hopes up and attracts the hand and favor of God in their lives and situations. I know it's way easier said than done, especially when you've gone through pain, loss, disappointment, hurt, and trauma, as we've experienced. It's hard. It's really hard, but God didn't call us to a life of ease and comfort.

Hope Against Hope (David) ✳━━━━━━━━━━━━━━━

If we go back to Abraham and Sarah's story, we know they had a happy ending. We know that they received their miracle child and that the promise from God did come to pass. It's easy for us to read their story

---

[31] Bill Johnson, Bethel, "Join Us LIVE | Bethel Church," July 17, 2022, https://www.youtube.com/watch?v=lbUZk98T0l0.

from our perspective and miss the impact of the hope they had to grab onto seemingly from thin air. To me, this is one of the most fascinating verses in all of Scripture: "In hope against hope he believed, so that he might become a father of many nations according to that which had been spoken, 'So shall your descendants be'" (Rom. 4:18 NASB).

Other translations put the phrase, "hope against all hope." Abraham was in hope against hope because he saw absolutely nothing in the natural that would lead him to believe that he and Sarah were going to bear a child. He was getting older and older. It was against the very nature of hope for him to hope. Did you catch that? For most of us to hope, there has to be a glimmer of something to hold on to. For me to hope that the Vikings win the Super Bowl, I naturally have to see them in the playoffs first. Abraham was hoping his "Vikings would win the Super Bowl" when they were 0 and 17 and not in the first round of the playoffs.

This applies to us as believers today! In our weakness, we only hope if we see evidence. Many of us only hope if we've seen it happen before or if a precedence is set. Is it possible we don't see the miracles and breakthroughs we are destined for because we haven't learned to hope against all hope? If this is the case, we haven't learned to trust what God said, even if all our circumstances look like the exact opposite.

Abraham would've looked like a crazy person if he stepped in our churches or Christian circles today—at least most of them. He'd probably be labeled the crazy prophetic guy who took things out of context. I imagine people would try to talk him out of the promise and suggest that maybe God's promise was a symbol for something else and not literal. Friends, I hope this is striking a nerve. I hope it's offensive. We are forfeiting so many promises and breakthroughs in this life because we won't take the risk to hope again. It's more comfortable to criticize those people. How do people like Abraham have that kind of hope and faith? How can you and I cultivate that? I believe the answer lies in the previous verse: "(as it is written, 'I have made you a father of many nations') in the presence of Him whom he believed, that is, God, who gives life to the dead and calls into being things that do not exist" (Rom. 4:17 NASB).

Abraham was IN hope against hope. How is that even possible? It's because his hope was in God and not in circumstance. His hope was against itself because there was no natural reason to believe the promise of children. At the same time, Abraham was IN hope because he hoped in God. God's words go forth from the beginning of time and call things into existence that don't exist yet. At that time, it was Abraham's Isaac. At present, it's our promised children. It's the breakthrough you've been hoping for. I believe the key for us in this season is to get our hopes up because our hopes are in God and His words for us. Abraham was able to put his hope and faith in God because He heard His word. Isaiah 55:11 (AMP) says God's word does not return to Him void. We see from the beginning of time that what God speaks happens. It's plain and simple. Even things that didn't yet exist come into existence with one word from God.

It's essential to understand that these words can undoubtedly come from Scripture, but they are not limited to Scripture. Before you stone me or throw this book away, let me explain. I believe the Bible is God's inspired Word and is infallible. There's nothing wrong with it. It's complete. However, God also speaks (reveals Himself) in other ways. He will speak through anything, including other people, the Bible, music, nature, sports teams, and still, small voices. It's important to remember and to keep in mind that when God speaks in these ways, it will never contradict Scripture. When God reveals Himself in these ways, it offers more insight into situations that may or may not be directly covered in the Bible. For example, dating is not a topic expressly talked about in the Bible. But we can discern God's will in this area from Scripture, advice from godly friends, or the Spirit's nudging of what feels right or wrong.

If you study the original language of the New Testament, which is Greek (and some Aramaic), you'll see that there are two different words for God's word. The first is logos. Logos is the immovable Word of God.

It is another word for the Scriptures, God's written Word. It is and always should be the final authority. AND (I won't say but) there's another word for God's word: It's rhema. Rhema comes from a verb that means to speak. One example of where we see this in the New Testament is in Romans 10:17 (NASB): "So faith comes from hearing, and hearing by the word (*rhema*) of Christ."

Here's another crucial example. The sword of the spirit talked about in Ephesians 6:17 is the rhema word of God! Bill Hamon, in his book *Prophets, Pitfalls, and Principles: God's Prophetic People Today,* says it this way:

✸ A rhema is a word or an illustration God speaks directly to us, and it addresses our personal, particular situation. It is a timely, Holy Spirit-inspired word from the Logos that brings life, power, and faith to perform and fulfill it. Its significance is exemplified in the injunction to take the "sword of the Spirit, which is the word [rhema] of God" (Eph. 6:17). It can be received through others such as by a prophetic word, or be an illumination given to one directly in their personal meditation time in the Bible or in prayer.[32]

It's so essential in this concept of hope and hoping again. If we are to get our hopes up, we must go to war with the sword of our prophetic promises, just like Abraham did! That is the key that unlocks our ability to hope against hope because our hope is in the One who spoke and still speaks! If you are tracking with me, you are starting to see that a key theme in miracles is faith; faith is only possible with hope, and hope comes from both the logos AND the rhema word of God. We can put our hope in what God has said because He can literally create life from His words.

Some translations that are more like paraphrases emphasize that

---

[32] Bill Hamon, Prophets, Pitfalls, and Principles: God's Prophetic People Today (Destiny Image Publishers: Shippensburg, PA, 2021), 280.

words are constantly going forth out of God's mouth (Matt. 4:4 TPT). When I see this, I like to look at the original translated word "proceeds" here. It is *ekporeuomai*. It can mean to depart out of, go out, or to leave.[33] It also can mean to move freely. This isn't a past-tense word. It's a word that is put here to suggest that words, which in this passage is the rhema word, are still being spoken, and that's how we are to live. It's both/and.

I understand that you may be thinking that people abuse the prophetic and it is used to manipulate and control. You may even be thinking, "I've seen prophets who are wrong, or at least look to be incorrect in the present tense." I agree that all of that is true. However, I would argue that the prophetic is still vital today. Both truths can exist at the same time. Just because imperfect people wrongly use it does not mean we must throw out the baby with the bath water. To do so is to vastly diminish the way that God wants to create in and through us in this hour!

It is clear that the prophetic and prophecy are for the new covenant, which is the covenant in which we live! You don't have to look much further than 1 Corinthians 14:1 (NASB), where we are told to desire a prophetic gift earnestly. It's also talked about in Romans 12 and Ephesians 4. Even after studying those passages, some will conclude that it was only for the early apostles and that the gift went away when they did. I don't know how to read Ephesians 4 and conclude that our gifts from the Holy Spirit, including prophecy, would ever expire:

✳ He "ascended" means that he returned to heaven, after he had first descended from the heights of heaven, even to the lower regions, namely, the earth. The same one who descended is also the one who ascended above the heights of heaven, in order to begin the restoration and fulfillment of all things. And he has appointed some with grace to be apostles, and some with grace to be prophets,

---

[33] National Ann"Ἐκπορεύομαι," billmounce.com, accessed March 24, 2025, https://www.billmounce.com/greek-dictionary/ekporeuomai.uity Regulations

and some with grace to be evangelists, and some with grace to be pastors, and some with grace to be teachers. And their calling is to nurture and prepare all the holy believers to do their own works of ministry, and as they do this they will enlarge and build up the body of Christ. These grace ministries will function until we all attain oneness into the faith, until we all experience the fullness of what it means to know the Son of God, and finally we become one into a perfect man with the full dimensions of spiritual maturity and fully developed into the abundance of Christ. (Eph. 4:9–13 TPT)

If I can paraphrase the last paragraph, it essentially says that these gifts will expire once we all look exactly like Jesus. Obviously, we are not there yet, but the prophetic helps us move in that direction with hope and faith. I humbly share these little insights with you because I had to dive in deep like this when others would question and doubt.

I didn't have the luxury to doubt the rhema word of God in my life. My family, kids, and future generations were at stake. In our story and in your story, we always have to get to the place where we can hope again so that we can have faith. Hebrews 11:1 (ESV) says, "Now faith is the assurance of things hoped for, the conviction of things not seen." You have to hope before you can be assured of the things you hope for (faith). Additionally, "without faith it is impossible to please" God (Heb. 11:6 ESV). If we can't get to the place of hope, we can't please God.

In our journey to Havilah, I realized that hoping against hope was a way to worship God. There wasn't a reason in the natural to hope, but there was a rhema word from God that allowed us to yield and battle with it as with a sword. It doesn't matter whether you've been waiting for ten minutes or ten years. It doesn't matter what the doctor's report says or what happened last time. I believe the key to seeing miracles come to pass throughout Scripture and history is to hope against all hope!

Reflection:

~ What "suddenly" are you praying for in your life?

~ What "suddenly" moments have you experienced? Write them down and thank God for them!

Prayer:

Lord, thank You that You still do miracles. I ask for breakthrough in my life today. I lay down my timeline and desires before You. Thank You for bringing the suddenly into my life at the right time. I pray in Jesus's name. Amen.

STEWARDING BREATHROUGH AND SHARING YOUR TESTIMONY

Let each generation tell its children of your mighty acts;

let them proclaim your power.

— Psalm 145:4 NLT

Abraham left a legacy for generations, and you, too, can leave a legacy that honors God. Part of leaving a legacy is sharing your testimony and breakthroughs and telling the next generations what God has done. You do not have to wait to share a testimony until all the things God has spoken to you have come to pass. Share your middle and what your testimony looks like right now.

A "Test"-imony (Melody) *————————————————————

When we were in the middle of our journey, I felt like I didn't have a testimony to share. It felt like so many things had gone opposite of what God had said, discouraging me from sharing what God was doing in my life. But one day, as I was praying, the Holy Spirit spoke this clearly:

> You are in the middle of your testimony. You have been waiting to get to the destiny God has for you before you share your testimony, but God is saying the middle is your testimony! There is a test in the testimony. You are passing the test in the middle. You are moving forward and grabbing hold of what God has done in your life up to this point with the expectation that it is NOT done yet. You have a powerful testimony. People need to hear it. You have been through a purifying process, and God has said He is shaping you into the person He has always meant you to be—full of Him. Where there was resistance in your heart, there is now a teachable spirit; where there was fear, there is now peace. Where there was doubt, there is now belief. Keep sharing what God has done and is going to do. Have faith like a mustard seed. He can move mountains!

I knew this wasn't just for me but for others too. Maybe it's even for you as you read it right now! You are a walking, living testimony, and the world needs to hear what God has brought you through and done in your life. It's for someone else. The revelations that God gives us as we go through trials are to help others who will one day come into our path.

The beginning, middle, and end of our stories have an influence on generations to come.

Memorial Stones (Melody) *————————————————————

When the Israelites crossed over the Jordan River into the promised land, the Lord told them to place memorial stones at the bottom, remembering what He had done. This was to be a sign for generations to come:

✻ When the whole nation had crossed the Jordan, the Lord said to Joshua, "Choose twelve men, one from each tribe, and command them to take twelve stones out of the middle of the Jordan, from the very place where the priests were standing. Tell them to carry these stones with them and to put them down where you camp tonight." Then Joshua called the twelve men he had chosen, and said, "Go into the Jordan ahead of the Covenant Box of the Lord your God. Each one of you take a stone on your shoulder, one for each of the tribes of Israel. These stones will remind the people of what the Lord has done. In the future, when your children ask what these stones mean to you, you will tell them that the water of the Jordan stopped flowing when the Lord's Covenant Box crossed the river. These stones will always remind the people of Israel of what happened here. (Josh. 4:1–7 GNT)

It goes on to say:

The people crossed the Jordan on the tenth day of the first month and camped at Gilgal, east of Jericho. There Joshua set up the twelve stones taken from the Jordan. And he said to the people of Israel, "In the future, when your children ask you what these stones mean, you will tell them about the time when Israel crossed the Jordan on dry ground. Tell them that the Lord your God dried up the water of the Jordan for you until you had crossed, just as he dried up the Red Sea for us. Because of this everyone on earth will know how great the Lord's power is, and you will honor the Lord your God forever. (Josh. 4:19–24 GNT)

There are many other examples in the Bible when God used different articles as symbols to remind His people of His faithfulness. In your walk with God, may you constantly be reminded of how God has been with you. You might still find yourself waiting for some breakthroughs in your life. Now is the time to read stories from the Bible about how God broke through in countless situations that seemed impossible. Instead of reacting to what is, how about we start responding to what should be? Recount the ways God has been faithful to you in the past. Whether big or small. Let it build your faith and hope for what God still wants to do! I want to go down to the grave believing God's word will come to pass, even if I do not fully see it in this life, because chances are, generations after me will.

Sharing your testimony, even as it develops, brings glory and honor to God. It makes way for more breakthroughs to happen. If we follow His voice, there is no limit to where God can lead us if we refuse to be hindered by our past circumstances. Our "not yets" are where Heaven can invade. When it takes a long time to get your breakthrough in a certain area, it's generally in that area where your calling or anointing lies. God will give you more authority and freedom in that area! Whatever your hardest-fought battle is, go after it like David did with Goliath. Slay the giants in the land God has given you. If He has said it is yours, then go after it with Him. He will bring victory with His mighty hand!

✳	I love Matthew Henry's commentary about the memorial stones in Joshua 4:

The works of the Lord are so worthy of remembrance, and the heart of man is so prone to forget them, that various methods are needful to refresh our memories, for the glory of God, our advantage, and that of our children. God gave orders for preparing this memorial. The priests with the ark did not stir till ordered to move. Let none be weary of waiting, while they have the tokens of God's presence with them, even the ark of the covenant, though it be in the depths of adversity. Notice is taken of the honour put upon Joshua. Those are feared in the best manner, and to the best purpose, who make it appear that God is with them, and that they set him before them. It is the duty of parents to tell their children betimes of the words and works of God, that they may be trained up in the way they should go. In all the instruction parents give their children, they should teach them to fear God. Serious godliness is the best learning. Are we not called, as much as the Israelites, to praise the loving-kindness of our God? Shall we not raise a pillar to our God, who has brought us through dangers and distresses in so wonderful a way? For hitherto the Lord hath helped us, as much as he did his saints of old. How great the stupidity and ingratitude of men, who perceive not His hand, and will not acknowledge his goodness, in their frequent deliverances![34]

Always give thanks in testimony. Tell others of what God has done. Each testimony is a memorial stone for generations to hear about who God is.

Stewarding Breakthrough (Melody) ✶ ────────────

When we go through trials in our lives, we sometimes feel like some moments are wasted—our time, finances, dreams, etc. But God wastes nothing. Nothing is too far gone for God. Nothing is too hard for God to heal. Time spent waiting is not wasted. Days of waiting for your breakthroughs are days that God is bringing your character through the refiner's fire, making you pure and compassionate for others you will one day come to know or meet.

34

Chapter Twelve

Matthew Henry and Thomas Scott, *Matthew Henry's Concise Commentary* (Oak Harbor, WA: Logos Research Systems, 1997), Jos 4:1–20.

Your pain has a purpose, and your purpose leaves a legacy. Your legacy is for generations of people you may never meet. When we get to the restored earth and Heaven, I love to imagine how many people will have been influenced for God's kingdom because of our choices, the words we spoke, how we celebrated what God did, and our actions. *There are little seeds that come out of your story that others will grab hold of and plant in the garden of their heart.* What has been done for you that someone can grab ahold of and ask God to do it again?

Testimony increases faith for more! Stewarding a breakthrough brings more measures of breakthrough. If God brings healing out of His abundance, we need to tap into His abundance! We see what's wrong in our story, but God sees what is right. Steward breakthrough by getting to know God's nature. It's His nature to do it again. Maybe not in the same way, but He is always willing to bring another testimony into our lives! What we possess right now is according to our capacity to steward in the way that He would. There is always a difference between what is in our possession and what is in our account. We possess only what we can steward well. Stewardship involves grace and obedience.

The word testimony means witness or evidence of something. Jesus is our witness, and the evidence is God's gift to us. We are called to continue to run the race and persevere to the end. I believe this also means persevering toward God's promises. Do not get distracted by other people's stories, but stay focused on the path God has you on. Even good things can be distractions. The enemy will use things that seem innocent to distract you from stewarding your breakthroughs. We must celebrate what God has done and look forward to the new thing that He wants to do next. Be ready for the next thing. Be alert and ready! Be entwined with the Holy Spirit to recognize what God is up to.

Imagine telling children and other family members what God has done in your life! For me, it looks like salvation and forgiveness. It looks like God being my comforter, counselor, provider, healer, friend, and so much more. Each breakthrough in my life is a memorial stone representing how God showed up. Taking testimonies and declaring them over your life is powerful! If He can do it for us, He can do it for you.

Stewarding breakthrough means pulling tomorrow's healing into today. The reality is that Jesus saw a breakthrough wherever He went. He knew God always wins. Breakthrough is a grace on your life to create a new normal! We should expect to see and experience miracles, healing, and breakthroughs in our lives! When you receive a small measure of breakthrough, continue to press in for more. God wants a full breakthrough for you. Thank Him for what He has done and is doing. *Thankfulness creates a space to welcome a heavenly invasion.* Give thanks and use God's authority in you to declare His promises and Scripture over your body, family, and legacy.

As I look at our life and testimony, it's not perfect, but it's God's testimony!

How you live your life will affect future generations physically, mentally, emotionally, and spiritually. Victory is waiting: "They conquered him completely through the blood of the Lamb and the powerful word of his testimony. They triumphed because they did not love and cling to their own lives, even when faced with death" (Rev. 12:11 TPT).

Jesus Is the Spirit of Prophecy (David) ✷────────────

I love Revelation 19:10 (TPT): "The testimony of Jesus is the spirit of prophecy." If you study the original text, it could also be translated as the very essence of prophecy. In other words, what Jesus has already done sums up the prophetic. This is so encouraging to us! When we hear amazing testimonies and witness of Jesus, it is not only incredible, but it also points to the future! This verse is so simple, yet it's so profound. We believe Jesus is fully God and was fully man. This verse seems to emphasize His humanity over His divinity. It does not negate that He is entirely God, but the Holy Spirit reminds us of something important in this verse. Jesus went through the tests as a human, and He took our place! He felt pain, betrayal, loss, disappointment, and all the agony we could possibly imagine, and then some! It didn't look like it was ending how it was supposed to. It looked dark and tragic when He was dying on that cross. It looked like the words about Him weren't true and that His promises weren't coming to pass. Yet, He overcame! He claimed victory over sin and death, and in the face of the adversary's most vicious attack in all of history, Jesus won. He won for all of us.

That testimony, friends, is the essence of the prophetic. He won, so we can expect to win! It doesn't matter how dark or impossible your situation feels. I get it. In fact, at the time of writing this chapter, we are still in the middle of our test. It looks dark. Sometimes, it feels like we take a step forward and then two steps backward. However, I believe this with all my heart: Babies are God's idea for us. He spoke it, and He creates with His words. He's done it for countless people since the beginning of time, and He will do it for us!!! The testimony we've heard repeatedly about Sarah, Rebekah, Hannah, and probably millions of modern-day couples is a prophetic word for us to grab onto!

We should be careful when we hear testimonies because it's natural to feel defeated when we hear of others' breakthroughs. It's human nature, and we come to God with the attitude that says, "What have you done for me lately?"

It's easy to feel like you got left out or that God forgot about you. Sometimes, when we see others get a breakthrough, we assume that less must be available for us. It's a scarcity mindset. That is not how the kingdom works. In the kingdom, breakthrough attracts more breakthroughs. Instead of getting discouraged, jealous, or defeated when we hear of the victory of others, we have an opportunity to celebrate and partake in the breakthrough. When we receive the testimony with joy, it prophesies the "suddenly" into our lives and situations!

That is why it is so important to share every measure of breakthrough that we get! It is never because we earn or deserve it, but when we brag about God, others can tap into that testimony. Even if you feel like you're still in the middle, share what He's done. Your deposit of testimony gains interest in the kingdom for you and for others! He gave you a breakthrough to give it away! It's not for our comfort or glory; it's always unto worship of the King!

Give What You Have (David) ✳━━━━━━━━━━━━━━

One of the most important things to consider when we talk about stewarding breakthroughs, testimonies, or anything for that matter, is the kingdom principle of advancement. Whether you consider the parable of the talents in Matthew 25 or that the kingdom of Heaven is compared to a mustard seed in Matthew 13, you will see that the best way to guarantee that you keep something is to give it away and increase it. Your story or breakthrough may start small and seem insignificant. That's perfect. Throughout Scripture and history, the hand of God seems to be attracted to the little things that can bring Him great glory. Don't be afraid of losing. If you are going to fear anything, tremble at the thought of keeping what God has given you to yourself. The world may think that is wise and prudent, but God calls it evil, untrustworthy, and lazy (Matt. 25:24–26)!

It doesn't matter what or how much God has given us in material things or blessings. He's already given us everything with His life. Jesus says, "The one who faithfully manages the little he has been given will be promoted and trusted with greater responsibilities. But those who cheat with the little they have been given will not be considered trustworthy to receive more" (Luke 16:10 TPT). Many people naturally apply this verse to money, and that's certainly a good application. However, in this chapter's context, it can apply to the measure of breakthroughs and testimonies we receive. I believe that when we show God that we can glorify Him even in the middle, He gives us more because He trusts that we will use our increase for kingdom advancement.

Sometimes, all we have is a "Hallelujah." Sometimes, all we have is an "I still believe." As I write this chapter, Brandon Lake just released a single called "Hard Fought Hallelujah." It's such a timely song as I write these words. One lyric says I'll "keep on singing 'Til my soul catches up with my song."[35] I find a lot of healing and strength in music and worship. Another one of my anthems is "I Still Believe" by Bethel Music. It is the sweetest aroma of praise when we bring God worship and belief in the middle of our testimony. I picture Heaven filling with the sweetest fragrance when we do that with an authentic heart. Only then does Heaven invade earth, and we get more of what God has for us. Give it all back to God and others. Heaven has the most significant interest rates.

Let Heaven invade your process, and let God bring the "suddenly" into your life. Prepare your heart and mind for what God will do in you. It's about you becoming more like Jesus through this. It's about contending for the breakthroughs you know are available in the heavenly realms. It's about increasing your hope so much that when things do not happen as you thought, it leads you right back to the Father. It's about getting up repeatedly after being knocked down by the enemy and not giving in to his tactics. It's about stewarding the words God has spoken for generations. Your process of suddenly is on its way. Get ready. Open your hands of faith and hope to receive all that God is doing. A testimony will become a ripple effect spreading from one body of water to another. As it gains momentum in the spirit, the waves of restoration will not be stopped. Get ready for your process of suddenly!

---

[35] Brandon Lake and Jelly Roll, "Hard Fought Hallelujah," *Hard Fought Hallelujah,* Provident Label Group, 2025.

Reflection:

    ~   What is one way you can steward your testimony/ breakthroughs?

    ~   How will you share your testimony with others?

Prayer:

    Lord, help me to steward the promises yet to be fulfilled, the breakthroughs You have brought in my life, and the impact it will have on generations. Show me ways I can steward and share my testimony. I pray in Jesus's name. Amen.

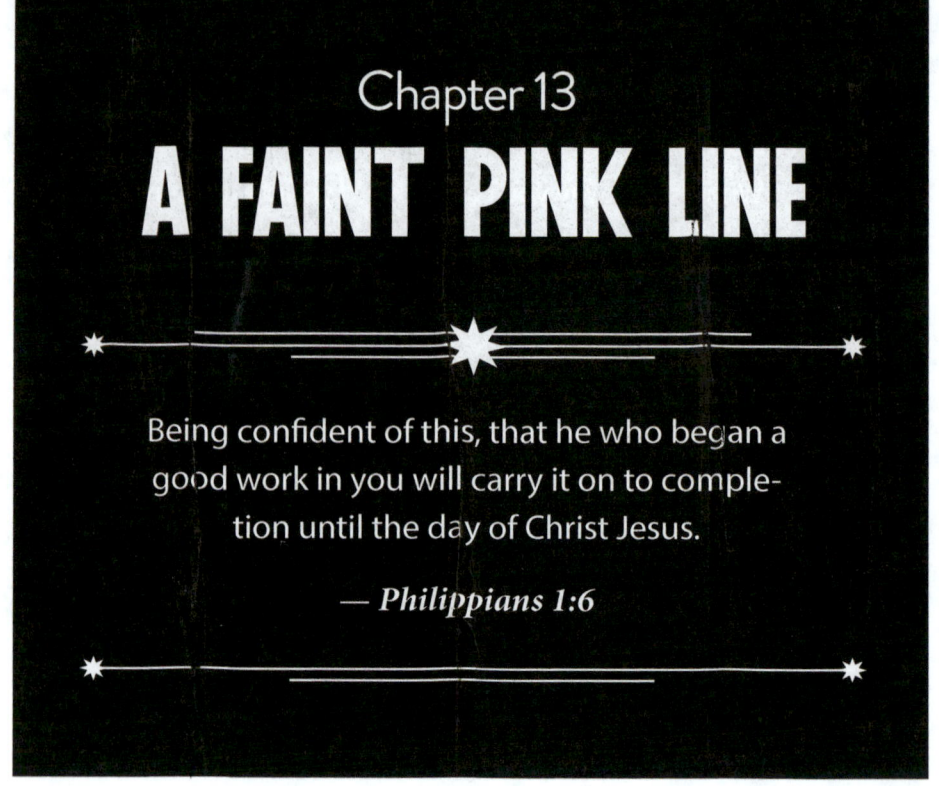

Chapter 13
A FAINT PINK LINE

Being confident of this, that he who began a good work in you will carry it on to completion until the day of Christ Jesus.

— *Philippians 1:6*

As you've read throughout this book, our journey with the Lord has been a roller coaster. On the one hand, we have positioned ourselves in such an expectant posture that we know God will move on our behalf and on your behalf for whatever you are believing for. On the other hand, we've been through the refiner's fire enough to know one thing: We are not God. There are no formulas that exist to get what we want. God is not a genie in Heaven granting wishes to us as His children. This is the tension and the mystery that we live in. We know babies are God's idea. We know (through Scripture and prophetic decrees) that He desires us to parent children. Yet, we see in the natural measures of breakthrough amid horrific pain, loss, and "not yets."

We've lived knowing that our God's goodness does not depend on our circumstances. He is only ever always good. Period. This is the process of suddenly we've been unpacking together throughout our lives and this book. The journey from the promise to the promised land involves wrestling with believing, forgiveness, grieving with hope, healing completely, hoping, and stewarding the breakthroughs we get. It involves praise and worship when it costs us something. It includes a sacrifice of praise when our natural beings want to do anything but praise.

Redeeming October (David) ✴━━━━━━━━━━━━━━━━━━

Then, something shifts—seemingly suddenly. From the outside looking in, it seems sudden, but you know, as well as anyone reading this, that a process of surrender led to the sudden breakthrough. God is with us through it all. I love the Holy Spirit. I know He didn't cause the trauma, tragedy, and heartache, but He has used it all to bring us to a place of intimacy with Him that we couldn't have received without the journey through pain.

We lost our first child—precious Esther—in October 2017. At the time of writing this chapter, it's 2025. It's been a nearly decade-long journey with life's most significant ups (Havilah) and most heartbreaking downs (Kanaan). Looking back, I sincerely don't know how we continued to have hope, faith, and belief in God and His promises. I have no answer other than it was supernatural grace. It still is—every day, every moment.

October 30, 2024, was a significant day for us. It wasn't significant because anything good happened, but our response showed me that we still had hope against all hope in this journey. We had exhausted all the options. We had tried everything imaginable. We went through all the natural healing modalities you could think of, as well as many of the medical ones. We experienced miscarriages, pregnancy, stillbirth, adoption, adoption failures, months in the NICU, and more. Yet, in our process of surrender, we still hadn't tried a fertility clinic that offered IUI/IVF treatments. It wasn't something we wanted to do or even something we thought we needed to do. We didn't want to manufacture our own miracle and "birth Ishmael," so to speak (Gen. 16).

However, we wanted to lay it all on the line and fully surrender our way of doing things. So, we did. We went in for a more traditional medical look at things and did another barrage of testing. They were looking deep for possible infections and other things that could have been preventing having healthy babies. October 30 was a scheduled test for Melody that would be painful and uncomfortable. There was one problem, though. She had a symptom that prevented her from doing the test. It was frustrating, and everything was delayed another month.

I'll spare you from details that aren't relevant, but this sparked a question and a wonder in me: Could we be pregnant? Could this be the suddenly unfolding in front of our very eyes? Was our surrender to a different idea enough to unlock a miracle we'd been praying for nearly a decade? I've documented this in my journal, confirming that we at least had a mustard seed of faith! We didn't want to get our hopes up. We didn't want to get heartbroken. But there was a supernatural grace, a gift of faith if you will, that begged the question: Is this the day of breakthrough? I prayed and prayed. I remembered a moment earlier in our story when God spoke to me and told me that He was redeeming the month of October! October wasn't over yet, and faith started to rise.

They ran blood pregnancy levels. It was negative. It felt cruel, and the enemy started attacking me with "I told you so" and "You shouldn't get your hopes up." Was I just a hopeless romantic who has this illusion that good things will happen even when there's no evidence? Or was I hearing from God? Either I'm crazy, or God still speaks. In that moment of torment and harassment from the enemy of my soul, I heard God speak again. He said: "I know this isn't the result you wanted. I'm sorry. I am God, and I AM STILL redeeming the month of October. I'm redeeming your whole story. I'm so proud of your faith, son."

I was brought back to my childhood when I was competing in wrestling. I would lose matches occasionally, and I took it hard. I don't like losing. I don't like losing wrestling matches or football games, and I don't like losing children. In one of those moments that was preparing me for more significant moments, my earthly daddy said to me: "Son, if you are ever wondering what I'm thinking of you when you see me in the bleachers, just know I'm only thinking one thought. I don't care if you win or if you lose, I couldn't be prouder of you."

I got up from my knees with a sense that we would win the next one. I believe our faith was counted as righteousness in God's eyes. Even though we didn't and don't handle every moment perfectly, He's so proud of our faith.

Hope Again (David) ✳━━━━━━━━━━━━━━━━━━━━━━━━━

Fast forward a few months, and we started encountering more pregnancy announcements. Some were less personal, and some were very intimate. Even though those moments were challenging, we felt the healing of parts of our hearts and souls and began celebrating with friends and family. The jealousy, envy, and comparison were subsiding. Yet, it was still natural to wonder if our turn would come. Another Vikings' season ended in tragedy, and I started to feel defeated again. Hoping again was hard, but hoping again was our only option.

We continued to do what we'd learned to do again and again. Forgive again. Hope again. Believe again. Pray again. Love again. Surrender again. Try again. In this season, we got a text message from a dear friend. He encouraged us prophetically that we are "noble warriors." That's what it felt like. This journey started to feel like a war. He described that God was putting shiny new armor on us and that we had renewed passion and excitement. We were reinvigorated. That word, like so many we've shared previously, was a lifeline. It was a dose of oxygen that burst into our spiritual lungs, allowing us to partner with God and breathe again! I'm in tears as I write this, but that day, a miracle happened. I don't have the space and time to unpack how important it is to have godly, spiritual friends. He lifted our arms like Aaron lifted Moses's arms, and together, we saw our enemies defeated and obstacles conquered.

Almost exactly two weeks from that day, it was time to take a pregnancy test. At this point in our journey, those moments have become challenging. We always have a glimmer of hope, but most times, if I'm being honest, those tests are thrown in the garbage with tears, pain, and dreams deferred. Melody was getting our daughter ready for the day, and I snuck a peek at the test in the bathroom. Nothing. I got in the shower with a heavy heart and pulled myself together for another day at work. As I was getting dressed, Melody said sheepishly, "Hey, I need you to look at this." I walked over, already knowing the result. "Do you see this?" she asked. There was an almost invisible pink line. It was so faint, but I couldn't deny that something was there. She took two more tests, and all of them came back with a faint pink line.

✳ It was like the cloud that Elijah's servant saw in 1 Kings 18:43–46 (ESV):

> And he said to his servant, "Go up now, look toward the sea." And he went up and looked and said, "There is nothing." And he said, "Go again," seven times. And at the seventh time he said, "Behold, a little cloud like a man's hand is rising from the sea." And he said, "Go up, say to Ahab, 'Prepare your chariot and go down, lest the rain stop you.'" And in a little while the heavens grew black with clouds and wind, and there was a great rain. And Ahab rode and went to Jezreel. And the hand of the Lord was on Elijah, and he gathered up his garment and ran before Ahab to the entrance of Jezreel.

There was a tiny cloud the size of a man's hand! There was a nearly invisible pink line. We knew God was looking for us to put our faith into action just like Elijah did. We went to the clinic to get a blood sample, but the results wouldn't come back until the next day.

God's Faithfulness (Melody) ✸━━━━━━━━━━━━━━

After having our daughter Havilah through adoption, we still couldn't shake the desire for more children and God's promises on our lives. Raising our daughter and seeing her grow each month was a joyful journey. It helped me to keep believing in God's words because she was a miracle I saw daily. We knew God was the only one who could bring another miracle into our family. We did what we knew to do in the natural and had to rest in what God was doing.

In December 2024, we sat down to have a typical conversation with our naturopathic doctor and OBGYN, discussing our next steps. We talked about what things we would address next and see what the new year would bring. It was an exciting time as we began to think and pray about being pregnant in the following months. We had expectant hope. We wanted to try naturally without IUI and see what God wanted to do. It would be four years since I became pregnant with our son Kanaan in January 2021. Being back on this timeline felt surreal, but we believed God would do a miracle in our family again. I was reminded that each testimony and breakthrough was a weapon against the enemy, and for us, our testimony was our children.

✸   Behold, children are a heritage from the Lord,
        the fruit of the womb a reward.
        Like arrows in the hand of a warrior
        are the children of one's youth.
        Blessed is the man
        who fills his quiver with them!
        He shall not be put to shame
        when he speaks with his enemies in the gate. (Ps. 127:3–5)

God was not done writing our story; we felt so sure of it. Constant reminders and confirmations from God made it evident that His fight for our family would bring victory. There was endurance that was needed on our part and a continued belief that God was faithful. After hearing more pregnancy announcements, we could tell our attitudes and hearts were different this time. We were genuinely happy for those people. Yes, we wanted it to, but we could honor what God was doing in others' lives.

We took a couple of risks without having to do IUI or IVF, and on January 30, we saw one dominant pink line and a faint one, but it was there! Two lines. A miracle in the works. I asked David if he could see them because I was shocked! Our faith increased, and we knew our dream would be confirmed the next day. We prayed and thanked God. It was happening! God remained faithful. We were expectant in faith for it to happen in January, and once it happened, it realigned our lives once again to God's faithfulness.

God always comes through on His word. He is waiting for us to partner with the better word that He speaks. We look forward to all God has in this pregnancy and child because it was His idea! He brought His blood-bought victory to fruition in our lives. We are overjoyed to have this gift! We pray the same for you, however that comes. Whether it be naturally, through IVF, through donor eggs, adoption, etc. These are each a miracle. There are no lesser miracles in God's kingdom. God knows exactly the path He wants you to take.

Surrender to the Process (David)

I remember Melody sending me a voicemail from the clinic. I was at work, so I went to the bathroom to listen to it. I heard the nurse say, "Your blood levels are consistent with early pregnancy. Congratulations!" I fell to my knees and worshiped on the bathroom floor!

Only God can come through suddenly like this in His perfect timing. It was so perfect that we got to finish this book with our suddenly and encourage you that yours is coming! You can ask our editor. We told her that we were believing by faith that we'd get to add another chapter. She was gracious and believed with us. We wrote this entire book in the middle of our journey by faith. We had already handed our manuscript to our editor, and God showed up in power.

Whatever it is that you are believing for and contending for, take this testimony as your own. Revelation 19:10 (ESV) says: "For the testimony of Jesus is the spirit of prophecy."

Surrender to the process. God does the suddenly! We are praying over every person who reads this. I release our testimony over you. May you experience the suddenly of God's breakthrough as you lean into His process!

PRAYERS AND DECLARATIONS

Prayer is communicating directly to God in praise, thanksgiving, repentance, and intercession. Declarations are faith and biblical statements regarding God's promises, our identity in Him, and our abilities. Declarations renew our minds!

Below are examples of some prayers and declarations we created to help you in your journey of having a family. You will find our thoughts on prayer and declarations that come from Scripture. We hope this will help remind you of God's healing power and hope!

In our humble opinion, declarations are an essential part of our breakthrough. They are a big part of the process that leads to sudden breakthroughs. Unfortunately, there are some reading this who probably cringed when you saw the word "declaration." I get it! I really do. Just like many things in the Christian faith, declarations have been perverted and misused by some for personal gain. However, the same can be said about any spiritual discipline. People have and will always use Scripture in a way that benefits them. Some people pray "selfishly." The prophetic can also be used in an unworthy manner. People can go after healing in a way that distorts the truth and makes people uncomfortable. All of this is and can be accurate, but just because some imperfect people misuse things does not mean that these things aren't and can't be important aspects of our spiritual journey with Jesus. In fact, the enemy will always try to distort what God does. I believe that one of the enemy's greatest weapons is this "paint with a broad stroke" strategy that suggests that if one person or movement gets it wrong, we must throw out the idea altogether. I refuse to align with that way of thinking. It makes my skin crawl because it creates unnecessary division in the body of Christ. If the enemy can distract us as the body by getting us to argue about petty theological things, we won't unite and focus on our ultimate responsibility: the great commission. What if we pooled all our resources together that are aimed at bashing other Christian movements and people and aimed them at reaching people with the gospel?

We have to be so careful when we attack other Christians because it waters down our witness. On the specific topic of declarations, I hear people reject it because somebody else misused it. Let me ask you this: Do we reject food because some people eat unhealthy? Do we reject marriage because some people get divorced? Do we reject preaching the gospel because some people don't accept it immediately? Of course not! Those are silly rhetorical questions.

I do not believe that "name it and claim it," or "blab it and grab it" teachings are biblically sound. I understand why some, including myself, get turned off by declarations because of those types of teachings. Scripture does not suggest that we can make things up out of thin air and just start to speak them to help them come to pass. That is a slippery slope that can lead to some dark spiritual places. We don't use declarations to get fancy cars or houses or to live an earthly life of luxury. There is nothing wrong with those things in and of themselves, but the correct focus of declarations is to partner with God to advance His kingdom in our spheres of influence and around the world! In fact, there is biblical precedence for declarations being used to partner with what God is doing. We've written about these examples laboriously, so I won't expound too much, but I wanted to bring them up in the light of making declarations.

In Genesis, God changes Abram and Sarai's names to Abraham and Sarah. The timing of this is critical. God changes their names before they see their promises come to pass! I believe He does this to get them to declare the promise in faith before they see it happen with their natural eyes. Abraham's name was changed to literally mean "father of multitudes" before it happened. Abraham and others around him started to declare the promise of many children because of that name change. Sarai and Sarah seem to mean similar things on the surface. It's a bit complicated in the original Hebrew, but in my studies, Sarah seems to more closely mirror our word for queen than princess, as we mentioned in an earlier chapter.

I realize that might seem like a minor detail, but it's not! Her name was changed to queen before she became the mother of Isaac! She stepped into her palace and destiny by partnering with God through declarations.

Even Jesus did this before He began His earthly ministry. I believe anything in the Bible is absolute truth, but when Jesus does something, it provides a model for us. Don't take my word for it. Here is Luke 4:18–21:

✸ The Spirit of the Lord is on me,
  because he has anointed me
  to proclaim good news to the poor.
  He has sent me to proclaim freedom for the prisoners
  and recovery of sight for the blind,
  to set the oppressed free,
  to proclaim the year of the Lord's favor.
  Then he rolled up the scroll, gave it back to the attendant and sat down. The eyes of everyone in the synagogue were fastened on him. He began by saying to them, "Today this scripture is fulfilled in your hearing."

Jesus reads a prophetic word about His destiny and then declares in verse 21: "Today this scripture is fulfilled in your hearing."

Follow Jesus. We've taken this model, and I encourage you to take it on your journey. Find Scripture and/or prophetic words about you and declare them over yourself, your family, and your situation. Remember, it's not about earthly comfort and gain; it's about finding God's "yes" over your life and coming into agreement and alignment with it!

Prayer for Conception ✸

Lord, we come before You, knowing that babies are Your idea. We believe that You created us to be fruitful. We ask for that fruitfulness to come to fruition right now. We ask that You would bring life into our bodies right now. Bring the perfect egg and sperm together. Let anything that stands in the way of that be cast down in Jesus's name. We call forth the miracle of conception today in Jesus's name.

✳ *Scripture Reference Reminders*
~ Psalm 34:5
~ Proverbs 3:5–6
~ Jeremiah 1:5
~ Mark 5:25–34
~ Philippians 4:6–8

✳ *Declarations for Conception*
~ My body will ovulate according to the right timing.
~ Our egg and sperm receive each other and form into a healthy child.
~ My womb is a safe place.
~ Any past trauma I cast out and replace with peace and health right now.
~ I believe I will conceive at the right time with the right hormone levels.
~ My body is not broken, and God created me to be fruitful.

Prayer for Fertility ✳
Lord, thank You for creating us in mind to be fruitful. We give thanks for the ways You have created our bodies and ask that You would bring healing to our bodies so we do not experience infertility any longer. We command (whatever diagnosis or condition) to be healed in Jesus's name right now. We command our bodies to align with the patterns of Heaven and come under Your authority, Lord. Thank You for making our bodies fertile and ready to produce fruit. We pray in Jesus's name. Amen.

✳ *Scripture Reference Reminders*

- ~ Genesis 25:19–26
- ~ Genesis 29:30–31:3
- ~ Genesis 30:17–22
- ~ Genesis 30:20–25
- ~ Genesis 35:23–26
- ~ Judges 13
- ~ 1 Samuel 1:1–28
- ~ 2 Kings 4:8–17
- ~ Psalm 113:9
- ~ Luke 1:5–20
- ~ Luke 1:36–37
- ~ Romans 4:16–24
- ~ Hebrews 11:11–12

✳ *Declarations for Fertility*

- ~ Infertility, loss, and sickness are not my identity, and I no longer accept them!
- ~ I am healed today because of what Jesus did.
- ~ I will not let any return of symptoms bring fear.
- ~ I will focus on God's Word to be fruitful and multiply.
- ~ My body was created in God's image.
- ~ Babies are God's idea.
- ~ My husband or wife is fertile, and they walk in health.
- ~ My union with (your spouse's name) is designed to bear fruit.
- ~ There is greatness in our DNA (because God put it there).

Prayer for Protection from Loss ✳━━━━━━━━━━

Thank You, Lord, for the opportunity to carry healthy babies to term. We ask that You bring protection from any kind of loss as well as loss we have experienced in the past. We surrender our worries and fears and ask You to bring us peace. Protect our minds and our hearts. Strengthen our bodies to carry life. Any loss that has happened with trauma we cast down and say no more. Jesus, we believe each life is precious and is Yours. We believe for healthy children. We pray in Jesus's name. Amen.

✶ *Scripture Reference Reminders*

Genesis 49:25

Exodus 23:25–26

Psalm 139:13–16

Proverbs 4:20–23

Zechariah 8:12

Galatians 3:13

2 Timothy 1:7

Hebrews 13:5

✶ *Declarations for Protection from Loss*

~ I no longer partner with (name the diagnosis, sickness, or issue). It has no place in my body, and I do not receive the reports.

~ I receive the full work of Christ.

~ I receive healing today.

~ I will walk in victory today because God has already won.

~ I walk in full health and wellness.

~ I do not partner with any lies that try to steal my healing.

~ I believe God's will is always to heal.

~ Jesus's broken body makes mine whole.

~ The blood of Jesus cleanses me.

Prayer for a Healthy Pregnancy ✶───────────────

Lord, thank You for creating my womb to be a safe place. Thank You that You help provide what my child needs as they grow. I ask for healing from aches and pains, morning sickness, and (list any other specific issues you are facing). Thank You for taking the place for all our suffering. We ask that You would be glorified through this pregnancy and that this child would be kept safe and grow as You have created him or her to. Let this child's body receive all the nutrients and development needed. We pray against anything that would come against having a peaceful and healthy pregnancy, in Jesus's name. Amen.

✹ *Scripture Reference Reminders*
- ~ Job 12:10
- ~ Psalm 22:9–10
- ~ Psalm 127:3
- ~ Psalm 139:13–16
- ~ Isaiah 40:31
- ~ Isaiah 53:5
- ~ James 1:17

✹ *Declarations for a Healthy Pregnancy*
- ~ I will not let fear or worry control my pregnancy.
- ~ I will have a healthy and comfortable pregnancy.
- ~ I can enjoy every aspect of my pregnancy.
- ~ I can have joy for the child I am carrying despite what the doctors or tests say.
- ~ I cast down morning sickness, pains, and aches in Jesus's name.
- ~ My child will grow to the right weight and development.
- ~ God will help me find the best doctor, nurses, doula, or midwife to work with.

Prayer for a Healthy Birth and Recovery ✳━━━━━━━━

Thank You, Lord, for the opportunity to carry this child and have a healthy delivery. I ask that You would be with me every step of the way in the birthing and recovery process. Help me to trust Your plan during the appointments, ultrasounds, and birth. I ask for protection for my body to be able to give birth safely and effectively. Help us to have the best nurses, doctors, or midwives with us. Let the recovery process be smooth and quicker than expected. We also ask for a supernatural birth without pain or emergencies. Thank You, God, for working out all the details. We pray in Jesus's name. Amen.

✳ *Scripture Reference Reminders*

- ~ Ecclesiastes 8:5–6
- ~ Isaiah 40:29, 31
- ~ Isaiah 53:4–5
- ~ Isaiah 65:23
- ~ Isaiah 66:7–9
- ~ Jeremiah 30:17
- ~ Galatians 3:13 (Jesus redeemed us from all curses)
- ~ Ephesians 6:10
- ~ Philippians 4:13

✳ *Declarations for a Healthy Birth and Recovery*

- ~ I will have no fear of the birth process.
- ~ My body was created to birth naturally.
- ~ God can help me birth supernaturally and without pain.
- ~ I can do this!
- ~ God is with me through my labor, contractions, and delivery.
- ~ My baby will come into the world healthy and vibrant.
- ~ I will recover smoothly and quickly after this birth.

~ I will rejoice over the birth of this child.

Before we conclude this book, we believe it is so crucial to understand what having a relationship with God means. John 3:16 says, "For God so loved the world that he gave his one and only son, that whoever believes in him shall not perish but have eternal life." This is good news! God loves us no matter what, and Jesus is the way to Father God. Without Him, we cannot have the relationship with God we were meant to have!

We must recognize that we are sinners in need of a Savior and that sin separates us from God. Romans 6:23 says, "The gift of God is eternal life." When we recognize our sin, repent, ask for forgiveness, and believe that Jesus is the only way to God, we can be born again! When you ask Christ to become your Lord and Savior, He will be with you forever. You will be forgiven and start a new life in Christ! If you have not done this for yourself, you have an opportunity. Starting a new life in Christ will be the best decision you have ever made. If you want to pray this prayer for the first time today, below is a simple prayer you can pray. Welcome to the kingdom family!

Prayer for Salvation ✳━━━━━━━━━━━━━━━━━━━━━

Lord, I recognize that I am a sinner in need of a Savior. I am done trying to strive and run my life the way I want. I repent of the things I have said, done, or thought that have not glorified You. I ask for forgiveness in everything. I believe that Jesus is the only way to the Father, and I believe that He died on the cross not just to save me from sin but to bring new life in me. I receive that new life today. Thank You, Jesus, for becoming the sacrifice for all of us. I thank You for Your Holy Spirit and healing my life, starting today. Show me how to live for You. I declare I am saved, healed, and delivered in Jesus's name!

Here are some Scripture references to help you get started on your new journey!

~ John 1:9–10
~ John 1:12
~ John 3:16
~ Romans 5:1
~ Romans 6:23

FERTILITY, LOSS, AND MISCARRIAGE SUPPORT

If you are in the same boat that we were in, you are probably wondering what practical steps you can take to improve your fertility and steward your body. We understand that, and so we have created a free resource on the QR code below that will take you to our website. It's a gift from us. We hope it helps you navigate to a better and healthier lifestyle as you grow your family together.

As we shared throughout our book, any kind of loss is painful and difficult. In our experience, there was not a lot of information out there on how to take care of your body physically after a loss. We are also sharing a free guide we created with the QR code below on our website. It's filled with tips and advice if you have recently experienced a loss or know someone who has. Taking care of ourselves is the last thing we think about when we have gone through the loss of a child. As hard as it may feel, taking care of ourselves is crucial for us, our marriage, and our families. May this resource be helpful to you as you start your process of healing.

NOTES